50 Amish Cooking Recipes for Home

By: Kelly Johnson

Table of Contents

- Amish Friendship Bread
- Chicken Corn Soup
- Ham Loaf
- Baked Corn Casserole
- Shoofly Pie
- Soft Pretzels
- Apple Butter
- Chicken Pot Pie
- Amish Potato Salad
- Peanut Butter Spread
- Pickled Beets
- Apple Dumplings
- Beef and Noodles
- Amish Cinnamon Bread
- Hamburger Casserole
- Whoopie Pies
- Amish White Bread
- Corn Fritters
- Dutch Meatloaf
- Amish Baked Oatmeal
- Lemon Sponge Pie
- Chicken and Biscuits
- Amish Peanut Butter Pie
- Church Spread
- Amish Egg Noodles
- Pennsylvania Dutch Funnel Cake
- Chicken Corn Pie
- Apple Slaw
- Homemade Root Beer
- Dutch Meatballs
- Amish Broccoli Salad
- Zucchini Bread
- Pork and Sauerkraut
- Molasses Cookies
- Chicken Salad
- Amish Pot Roast

- Red Beet Eggs
- Baked Apples
- Beef Stew
- Amish Cheese Ball
- Shaker Chicken and Dumplings
- Black Raspberry Jam
- Pumpkin Whoopie Pies
- Amish Wedding Cake
- Scalloped Corn
- Chicken Fingers
- Rhubarb Custard Pie
- Sloppy Joes
- Amish Macaroni Salad
- Baked Chicken

Amish Friendship Bread

Starter Ingredients:

- 1 cup all-purpose flour
- 1 cup granulated sugar
- 1 cup milk

Bread Ingredients:

- 1 cup Amish Friendship Bread starter (from above)
- 1 cup vegetable oil
- 1 cup granulated sugar
- 3 large eggs
- 2 cups all-purpose flour
- 1 1/2 tsp baking powder
- 1/2 tsp baking soda
- 1/2 tsp salt
- 2 tsp ground cinnamon
- 1-2 boxes instant vanilla pudding mix (optional, for added flavor)
- 1 cup chopped nuts, raisins, or chocolate chips (optional)

Cinnamon Sugar Topping (optional):

- 1/2 cup granulated sugar
- 1 1/2 tsp ground cinnamon

Instructions:

Day 1: Making the Starter

1. In a large glass or plastic bowl (not metal), combine 1 cup flour, 1 cup sugar, and 1 cup milk. Stir until well combined.
2. Cover loosely with a clean cloth or plastic wrap. Do not use airtight containers as the mixture needs to breathe.
3. Leave the mixture at room temperature.

Days 2-4: Stir the Starter

- Stir the mixture with a wooden spoon or spatula once a day.

Day 5: Feed the Starter

1. Add 1 cup flour, 1 cup sugar, and 1 cup milk to the starter. Stir until well combined.
2. Stir once a day for the next 4 days.

Day 10: Use and Share the Starter

1. Pour 1 cup of the starter into a separate container to use for baking.
2. Give the remaining starter to friends along with the instructions for Days 1-10, or discard it if you don't want to continue the cycle.

Bread Instructions:

1. Preheat your oven to 325°F (165°C). Grease two 9x5-inch loaf pans.
2. In a large bowl, combine the 1 cup of Amish Friendship Bread starter, vegetable oil, 1 cup sugar, and eggs. Mix well.
3. In a separate bowl, whisk together 2 cups flour, baking powder, baking soda, salt, and cinnamon. Gradually add the dry ingredients to the wet ingredients, stirring until just combined. Do not overmix.
4. If desired, fold in vanilla pudding mix and chopped nuts, raisins, or chocolate chips for added flavor and texture.
5. Divide the batter evenly between the prepared loaf pans.
6. If using the cinnamon sugar topping, mix together 1/2 cup sugar and 1 1/2 tsp cinnamon. Sprinkle evenly over the batter in the loaf pans.
7. Bake in the preheated oven for 45-50 minutes, or until a toothpick inserted into the center of the loaves comes out clean.
8. Allow the bread to cool in the pans for 10 minutes before removing to wire racks to cool completely.
9. Slice and enjoy!

Notes:

- The Amish Friendship Bread starter can be kept going indefinitely by following the feeding instructions every 10 days.
- Feel free to customize the bread with your favorite additions like nuts, dried fruit, or chocolate chips.
- This bread is best enjoyed fresh but can be stored in an airtight container at room temperature for up to 3 days or frozen for longer storage.

Amish Friendship Bread is not just a delicious treat but also a wonderful tradition of sharing and community. Enjoy baking and sharing this special bread with your loved ones!

Chicken Corn Soup

Ingredients:

- 1 lb boneless, skinless chicken breasts or thighs, diced
- 1 onion, finely chopped
- 2 carrots, diced
- 2 celery stalks, diced
- 1 red bell pepper, diced (optional)
- 2 cloves garlic, minced
- 6 cups chicken broth
- 2 cups frozen or fresh corn kernels
- 1 cup heavy cream or half-and-half
- 1/4 cup all-purpose flour
- 2 tbsp butter
- 1 tsp dried thyme (or 1 tbsp fresh thyme leaves)
- Salt and pepper, to taste
- Fresh parsley, chopped (for garnish)
- Crusty bread, for serving

Instructions:

1. **Cook the Chicken:**
    - In a large pot or Dutch oven, melt the butter over medium heat. Add the diced chicken and cook until browned on all sides, about 5-7 minutes. Remove the chicken from the pot and set aside.
2. **Sauté Vegetables:**
    - In the same pot, add the chopped onion, carrots, celery, and red bell pepper (if using). Sauté until the vegetables are softened, about 5 minutes.
    - Add the minced garlic and cook for another minute until fragrant.
3. **Make the Soup Base:**
    - Sprinkle the flour over the vegetables and stir to coat evenly. Cook for 1-2 minutes to remove the raw flour taste.
    - Gradually pour in the chicken broth, stirring constantly to prevent lumps. Bring to a boil, then reduce the heat to low.
4. **Add Chicken and Corn:**
    - Return the cooked chicken to the pot. Add the corn kernels and dried thyme. Stir to combine.
    - Simmer the soup uncovered for 15-20 minutes, or until the chicken is cooked through and the vegetables are tender.
5. **Thicken the Soup:**
    - In a small bowl, whisk together the heavy cream (or half-and-half) with 1/4 cup of soup broth from the pot until smooth. Gradually pour the cream mixture back into the pot, stirring continuously.

- Continue to simmer for another 5-10 minutes, stirring occasionally, until the soup has thickened slightly.
6. **Season and Serve:**
    - Taste the soup and season with salt and pepper as needed.
    - Ladle the Chicken Corn Soup into bowls and garnish with chopped fresh parsley.
    - Serve hot with crusty bread on the side.

Tips:

- **Variations:** You can add diced potatoes or diced tomatoes for additional texture and flavor.
- **Cream Substitution:** If you prefer a lighter version, you can substitute the heavy cream with whole milk or low-fat milk, though the soup won't be as rich.
- **Storage:** Chicken Corn Soup can be stored in the refrigerator for up to 4 days. Reheat gently on the stove before serving.

Enjoy this comforting Chicken Corn Soup as a satisfying meal on its own or as a starter to a larger meal. It's perfect for chilly days and guaranteed to warm you up from the inside out!

Ham Loaf

Ingredients:

- 2 lbs ground ham
- 1 lb ground pork (or ground beef)
- 1 cup breadcrumbs
- 2 eggs, beaten
- 1/2 cup milk
- 1 onion, finely chopped
- 1/2 cup green bell pepper, finely chopped
- 1/2 cup celery, finely chopped
- 1/4 cup ketchup
- 2 tbsp brown sugar
- 1 tbsp mustard (prepared mustard)
- 1 tsp Worcestershire sauce
- 1/2 tsp black pepper
- Salt, to taste

Glaze Ingredients:

- 1/2 cup ketchup
- 1/4 cup brown sugar
- 1 tbsp mustard

Instructions:

1. **Preheat Oven:**
    - Preheat your oven to 350°F (175°C). Grease a loaf pan or baking dish.
2. **Prepare the Ham Loaf Mixture:**
    - In a large bowl, combine the ground ham and ground pork (or beef).
    - Add breadcrumbs, beaten eggs, milk, chopped onion, green bell pepper, and celery. Mix well until thoroughly combined.
3. **Season the Mixture:**
    - Stir in the ketchup, brown sugar, mustard, Worcestershire sauce, black pepper, and salt to taste. Mix until all ingredients are evenly incorporated.
4. **Shape the Loaf:**
    - Transfer the mixture into the greased loaf pan or baking dish. Press the mixture firmly into the pan, shaping it into a loaf shape.
5. **Make the Glaze:**
    - In a small bowl, whisk together the ketchup, brown sugar, and mustard until smooth. Spread the glaze evenly over the top of the ham loaf.
6. **Bake the Ham Loaf:**

- Bake in the preheated oven for 1 to 1.5 hours, or until the internal temperature reaches 160°F (71°C) and the loaf is cooked through.
- If the glaze starts to brown too quickly, cover loosely with foil during the last 30 minutes of baking.

7. **Rest and Serve:**
    - Remove the ham loaf from the oven and let it rest for 10 minutes before slicing.
    - Slice and serve warm, garnished with additional glaze if desired.

Tips:

- **Variations:** Some recipes may include additional ingredients like crushed pineapple or mustard sauce for added flavor.
- **Storage:** Leftover ham loaf can be stored in an airtight container in the refrigerator for up to 3 days. Reheat gently in the oven or microwave before serving.
- **Serve with:** Ham loaf pairs well with mashed potatoes, steamed vegetables, or a side salad.

Enjoy this classic ham loaf recipe, perfect for a comforting family meal or a holiday gathering. It's a delicious way to enjoy the flavors of ham in a new and savory dish!

Baked Corn Casserole

Ingredients:

- 2 cans (15 oz each) whole kernel corn, drained
- 1 can (15 oz) cream-style corn
- 1 cup sour cream
- 1/2 cup (1 stick) unsalted butter, melted
- 1 package (8.5 oz) corn muffin mix (such as Jiffy)
- 2 eggs, beaten
- 1 cup shredded cheddar cheese (optional)
- Salt and pepper, to taste
- Chopped fresh parsley or chives, for garnish (optional)

Instructions:

1. **Preheat Oven:**
   - Preheat your oven to 350°F (175°C). Grease a 9x13-inch baking dish or casserole dish with butter or cooking spray.
2. **Mix Ingredients:**
   - In a large bowl, combine the whole kernel corn, cream-style corn, sour cream, melted butter, corn muffin mix, beaten eggs, and shredded cheddar cheese (if using). Mix until well combined.
   - Season with salt and pepper to taste.
3. **Bake the Casserole:**
   - Pour the corn mixture into the prepared baking dish, spreading it out evenly.
   - Bake in the preheated oven for 45-50 minutes, or until the top is golden brown and the center is set. The casserole should be slightly firm to the touch.
4. **Serve:**
   - Remove from the oven and let it cool for a few minutes before serving.
   - Garnish with chopped fresh parsley or chives if desired.
   - Serve warm as a side dish alongside roasted meats, grilled chicken, or as part of a holiday feast.

Tips:

- **Variations:** Add diced green chilies, diced bell peppers, or cooked crumbled bacon for extra flavor and texture.
- **Storage:** Leftover baked corn casserole can be stored in an airtight container in the refrigerator for up to 3 days. Reheat gently in the oven or microwave before serving.
- **Make Ahead:** You can assemble the casserole ahead of time and refrigerate it unbaked. Bake as directed when ready to serve.

Baked Corn Casserole is creamy, slightly sweet, and pairs well with a variety of main dishes. It's a versatile and comforting addition to any meal, sure to be a crowd-pleaser!

Shoofly Pie

Ingredients:

Pie Crust:

- 1 1/4 cups all-purpose flour
- 1/2 tsp salt
- 1/3 cup vegetable shortening or cold unsalted butter, cut into small pieces
- 4-5 tbsp ice water

Filling:

- 1 cup molasses (light or dark, according to preference)
- 3/4 cup boiling water
- 1 tsp baking soda
- 1 egg, beaten
- 1 cup all-purpose flour
- 1/2 cup packed light brown sugar
- 2 tbsp unsalted butter, melted

Instructions:

Pie Crust:

1. **Prepare the Crust:**
    - In a large mixing bowl, combine the flour and salt. Cut in the shortening or butter using a pastry cutter or your fingers until the mixture resembles coarse crumbs.
    - Add ice water, 1 tablespoon at a time, and mix with a fork until the dough begins to come together. Form the dough into a ball, wrap it in plastic wrap, and refrigerate for at least 30 minutes.
2. **Preheat Oven:**
    - Preheat your oven to 375°F (190°C).
3. **Roll Out the Crust:**
    - On a lightly floured surface, roll out the chilled dough into a circle about 12 inches in diameter. Carefully transfer the dough to a 9-inch pie dish. Trim and crimp the edges as desired.

Filling:

1. **Prepare the Filling:**
    - In a medium bowl, dissolve the baking soda in the boiling water. Stir in the molasses and beaten egg until well combined.
2. **Assemble the Pie:**

- In another bowl, combine the flour and brown sugar. Gradually add the melted butter, stirring with a fork until the mixture resembles coarse crumbs.
3. **Bake the Pie:**
    - Pour the molasses filling into the prepared pie crust.
    - Sprinkle the flour-brown sugar mixture evenly over the top of the filling.
    - Place the pie on a baking sheet to catch any drips and bake in the preheated oven for 45-50 minutes, or until the filling is set and the crust is golden brown.
4. **Cool and Serve:**
    - Remove the pie from the oven and let it cool completely on a wire rack before slicing.
    - Serve slices of Shoofly Pie at room temperature or slightly warmed, with a dollop of whipped cream or a scoop of vanilla ice cream if desired.

Tips:

- **Molasses:** You can use either light or dark molasses depending on your preference. Dark molasses will give the pie a richer, more robust flavor.
- **Storage:** Shoofly Pie can be stored covered at room temperature for up to 2 days. It can also be refrigerated for longer storage, though the crust may become slightly softer.
- **Variations:** Some recipes add a pinch of cinnamon or ginger to the flour-brown sugar topping for extra flavor.

Enjoy this classic Shoofly Pie recipe, a delightful treat that's perfect for sharing with family and friends, especially during holidays and gatherings!

Soft Pretzels

Ingredients:

- 1 1/2 cups warm water (110-115°F)
- 1 tbsp granulated sugar
- 2 tsp kosher salt
- 2 1/4 tsp active dry yeast (1 packet)
- 4 1/2 cups all-purpose flour
- 4 tbsp unsalted butter, melted
- Vegetable oil, for greasing
- 10 cups water
- 2/3 cup baking soda
- 1 large egg yolk, beaten with 1 tbsp water (for egg wash)
- Coarse salt or pretzel salt, for sprinkling

Instructions:

1. **Activate the Yeast:**
   - In a small bowl, combine warm water, sugar, and kosher salt. Sprinkle the yeast on top and let it sit for 5 minutes, or until foamy.
2. **Mix the Dough:**
   - In a large mixing bowl or the bowl of a stand mixer fitted with a dough hook, combine the flour and melted butter. Pour in the yeast mixture and knead until the dough is smooth and pulls away from the sides of the bowl, about 5-7 minutes.
3. **First Rise:**
   - Remove the dough from the bowl and lightly grease the bowl with vegetable oil. Place the dough back in the bowl, cover with a clean towel or plastic wrap, and let it rise in a warm place for 1 hour, or until doubled in size.
4. **Preheat Oven:**
   - Preheat your oven to 450°F (230°C). Line two baking sheets with parchment paper and lightly grease with oil.
5. **Prepare the Water Bath:**
   - In a large pot, bring 10 cups of water and baking soda to a rolling boil.
6. **Shape the Pretzels:**
   - Punch down the risen dough and divide it into 8 equal pieces. Roll each piece into a long rope, about 24 inches long.
   - Shape each rope into a pretzel: form a U-shape, then cross the ends over each other and press onto the bottom of the U to form the classic pretzel shape. Alternatively, you can simply twist them into pretzel sticks or other shapes.
7. **Boil the Pretzels:**
   - Carefully place each pretzel into the boiling water bath for 30 seconds, flipping once with a slotted spoon or spatula. Remove and place them on the prepared baking sheets, spacing them apart.

8. **Bake the Pretzels:**
    - Brush each pretzel with the beaten egg yolk wash and sprinkle with coarse salt or pretzel salt.
    - Bake in the preheated oven for 12-15 minutes, or until golden brown.
9. **Cool and Serve:**
    - Remove from the oven and let the pretzels cool slightly on a wire rack before serving.
    - Enjoy warm with mustard, cheese sauce, or your favorite dipping sauce!

Tips:

- **Variations:** You can sprinkle the pretzels with cinnamon sugar instead of salt for a sweet twist. Add shredded cheese on top before baking for cheesy pretzels.
- **Storage:** Soft pretzels are best enjoyed fresh on the day they are made. If you have leftovers, store them in an airtight container at room temperature and reheat in the oven for a few minutes to regain their freshness.

Homemade soft pretzels are a fun baking project that yields delicious results. They're perfect for snacking, parties, or even as a treat with your favorite beverage. Enjoy making and sharing these delightful treats!

Apple Butter

Ingredients:

- 5 lbs apples (such as Granny Smith, Honeycrisp, or a mix of sweet and tart varieties)
- 2 cups granulated sugar
- 1 cup brown sugar
- 1 tbsp ground cinnamon
- 1/2 tsp ground cloves
- 1/2 tsp ground nutmeg
- 1/4 tsp salt
- 1 tbsp vanilla extract (optional)

Instructions:

1. **Prepare the Apples:**
   - Wash, peel, core, and chop the apples into small chunks.
2. **Cook the Apples:**
   - In a large pot or Dutch oven, combine the chopped apples with both sugars, cinnamon, cloves, nutmeg, and salt.
   - Cook over medium heat, stirring frequently, until the apples begin to release their juices and soften, about 10-15 minutes.
3. **Simmer and Reduce:**
   - Reduce the heat to low and simmer the apple mixture uncovered, stirring occasionally to prevent sticking, for 1.5 to 2 hours. The mixture should thicken and darken to a deep brown color.
4. **Blend or Process (optional):**
   - For a smoother consistency, use an immersion blender directly in the pot or carefully transfer the mixture to a blender or food processor. Blend until smooth.
5. **Add Vanilla (optional):**
   - Stir in vanilla extract if using, and continue to cook for another 10-15 minutes to blend the flavors.
6. **Can or Store:**
   - If canning for long-term storage, follow proper canning procedures and process in a water bath for 10 minutes. Otherwise, let the apple butter cool completely before transferring it to clean, airtight containers or jars. Store in the refrigerator for up to 2 weeks or freeze for longer storage.

Tips:

- **Apples:** Choose apples that are good for cooking, such as Granny Smith or Honeycrisp, for a balance of sweetness and tartness.
- **Sweetness:** Adjust the amount of sugar to taste, depending on the sweetness of the apples and your preference.
- **Spices:** Feel free to adjust the spices according to your taste. Some recipes also include a pinch of cloves or allspice for added complexity.

- **Uses:** Apple butter is delicious spread on toast, biscuits, pancakes, or waffles. It can also be used as a topping for oatmeal, yogurt, or ice cream, and as an ingredient in baking recipes.

Homemade apple butter is a wonderful way to preserve the flavors of fresh apples and enjoy them throughout the year. It's a versatile and delicious addition to your pantry!

Chicken Pot Pie

Ingredients:

Pie Crust:

- 2 1/2 cups all-purpose flour
- 1 tsp salt
- 1 cup unsalted butter, chilled and cut into cubes
- 6-8 tbsp ice water

Filling:

- 2 tbsp unsalted butter
- 1 onion, finely chopped
- 2 carrots, diced
- 2 celery stalks, diced
- 2 cloves garlic, minced
- 1/2 cup all-purpose flour
- 2 cups chicken broth
- 1 cup whole milk or heavy cream
- 1 tsp dried thyme (or 1 tbsp fresh thyme leaves)
- Salt and pepper, to taste
- 3 cups cooked chicken, diced or shredded (rotisserie chicken works well)
- 1 cup frozen peas (optional)
- 1/2 cup frozen corn (optional)
- 1 egg, beaten (for egg wash)

Instructions:

Pie Crust:

1. **Prepare the Pie Crust:**
    - In a large bowl, whisk together the flour and salt. Add the chilled butter cubes and use a pastry cutter or your fingers to work the butter into the flour mixture until it resembles coarse crumbs.
    - Gradually add ice water, 1 tablespoon at a time, and mix with a fork until the dough begins to come together. You may not need to use all of the water.
    - Turn the dough out onto a lightly floured surface and divide it into two equal portions. Shape each portion into a disk, wrap tightly in plastic wrap, and refrigerate for at least 1 hour.

Filling:

1. **Prepare the Filling:**

- In a large skillet or Dutch oven, melt the butter over medium heat. Add the chopped onion, carrots, and celery. Cook until vegetables are softened, about 5-7 minutes.
- Add the minced garlic and cook for an additional 1 minute until fragrant.

2. **Make the Sauce:**
   - Sprinkle the flour over the vegetables and stir to coat evenly. Cook for 1-2 minutes to remove the raw flour taste.
   - Gradually pour in the chicken broth and milk or cream, stirring constantly to prevent lumps. Bring to a simmer and cook until the sauce thickens, stirring occasionally, about 5-7 minutes.
   - Stir in the dried thyme, salt, and pepper to taste.
3. **Assemble the Pie:**
   - Remove the sauce from heat and stir in the cooked chicken, frozen peas, and corn (if using). Mix until well combined.
4. **Preheat Oven:**
   - Preheat your oven to 400°F (200°C).
5. **Roll Out the Pie Crust:**
   - On a lightly floured surface, roll out one of the chilled pie dough disks into a circle large enough to fit your pie dish with some overhang.
6. **Fill the Pie:**
   - Transfer the chicken filling into the prepared pie dish. Spread it out evenly.
7. **Cover with Crust:**
   - Roll out the second pie dough disk into a circle slightly larger than the pie dish. Place it over the filling. Trim any excess dough and press the edges of the top and bottom crusts together to seal. Crimp the edges with a fork or your fingers.
8. **Ventilation and Egg Wash:**
   - Cut a few slits in the top crust to allow steam to escape during baking. Brush the top crust with beaten egg, which will give it a golden color when baked.
9. **Bake the Pie:**
   - Place the pie dish on a baking sheet (to catch any drips) and bake in the preheated oven for 30-35 minutes, or until the crust is golden brown and the filling is bubbly.
10. **Cool and Serve:**
    - Remove the chicken pot pie from the oven and let it cool for 10 minutes before slicing and serving.

Tips:

- **Vegetables:** Feel free to customize the vegetables based on your preference. Mushrooms, green beans, or diced potatoes can also be great additions.
- **Make-Ahead:** You can prepare the filling and crust ahead of time and assemble the pie just before baking. Alternatively, bake the pie and then freeze it (unbaked or baked) for later use.

- **Storage:** Leftover chicken pot pie can be stored covered in the refrigerator for 3-4 days. Reheat in the oven or microwave until warmed through.

Enjoy this homemade chicken pot pie, a classic comfort food that's perfect for chilly evenings or family gatherings!

Amish Potato Salad

Ingredients:

- 2 lbs potatoes (Yukon Gold or red potatoes work well)
- 1/2 cup mayonnaise
- 2 tbsp yellow mustard
- 2 tbsp apple cider vinegar
- 1/2 cup celery, finely chopped
- 1/2 cup red onion, finely chopped
- 1/4 cup sweet pickles or sweet pickle relish, chopped
- 2 hard-boiled eggs, chopped (optional)
- Salt and pepper, to taste
- Paprika, for garnish (optional)
- Chopped fresh parsley or chives, for garnish (optional)

Instructions:

1. **Cook the Potatoes:**
    - Wash and scrub the potatoes. Place them in a large pot and cover with cold water. Add a pinch of salt. Bring to a boil over medium-high heat, then reduce the heat to medium-low and simmer until the potatoes are tender when pierced with a fork, about 15-20 minutes.
    - Drain the potatoes and let them cool slightly.
2. **Prepare the Dressing:**
    - In a large bowl, whisk together the mayonnaise, mustard, and apple cider vinegar until smooth and well combined. Season with salt and pepper to taste.
3. **Assemble the Salad:**
    - Once the potatoes are cool enough to handle, peel (if desired) and cut them into bite-sized cubes. Add the cubed potatoes to the bowl with the dressing.
    - Add the chopped celery, red onion, sweet pickles or pickle relish, and chopped hard-boiled eggs (if using). Gently toss everything together until evenly coated with the dressing.
4. **Chill and Serve:**
    - Cover the potato salad and refrigerate for at least 1 hour to allow the flavors to meld together.
    - Before serving, garnish with a sprinkle of paprika and chopped fresh parsley or chives, if desired.

Tips:

- **Potato Varieties:** Yukon Gold potatoes are ideal for their creamy texture, but you can use red potatoes or russet potatoes if preferred.

- **Adjusting Consistency:** If the potato salad seems dry after chilling, you can add a bit more mayonnaise or a splash of apple cider vinegar to loosen it up.
- **Make-Ahead:** Amish Potato Salad tastes even better the next day after the flavors have had time to meld. It can be made up to 24 hours in advance and stored covered in the refrigerator.
- **Customization:** Some variations include adding diced bell peppers, dill pickles instead of sweet pickles, or a sprinkle of celery seed for extra flavor.

This Amish Potato Salad recipe is perfect for picnics, barbecues, or as a side dish for any meal. Its creamy texture and classic flavors are sure to be a hit!

Peanut Butter Spread

Ingredients:

- 2 cups dry roasted peanuts (unsalted)
- 1-2 tbsp honey or maple syrup (optional, for sweetness)
- 1-2 tbsp peanut oil or vegetable oil (optional, for smoother consistency)
- 1/2 tsp salt (optional, adjust to taste)

Instructions:

1. **Prepare the Peanuts:**
   - If using unsalted peanuts, you may want to roast them for enhanced flavor. Preheat your oven to 350°F (175°C). Spread the peanuts in a single layer on a baking sheet and roast for 8-10 minutes, stirring occasionally, until lightly golden and fragrant. Let them cool slightly.
2. **Process the Peanuts:**
   - Place the roasted peanuts in a food processor or high-powered blender. Blend for 1-2 minutes until the peanuts are finely ground and begin to clump together.
3. **Add Optional Ingredients:**
   - If desired, add honey or maple syrup for sweetness, oil for a smoother texture, and salt to taste.
4. **Blend Until Smooth:**
   - Continue blending the mixture for 3-5 more minutes, scraping down the sides of the processor or blender as needed, until the peanut butter reaches your desired consistency. If it seems too thick, you can add a bit more oil.
5. **Store and Serve:**
   - Transfer the peanut butter spread to a clean jar or airtight container. It can be stored at room temperature for up to 2 weeks, or longer in the refrigerator.
6. **Enjoy:**
   - Spread the homemade peanut butter on toast, use it as a dip for fruits or vegetables, or incorporate it into your favorite recipes.

Tips:

- **Variations:** You can customize your peanut butter spread by adding cocoa powder for chocolate peanut butter, cinnamon for a spiced version, or even mixing in chopped nuts or chocolate chips after blending.
- **Consistency:** Adjust the amount of oil based on your preference for a thicker or smoother peanut butter.
- **Nutritional Benefits:** Homemade peanut butter allows you to skip added sugars and preservatives often found in commercial brands, making it a healthier option.

Homemade peanut butter spread is versatile, delicious, and a great way to enjoy the natural flavor of peanuts with your favorite additions. It's perfect for snacks, sandwiches, and even baking!

Pickled Beets

Ingredients:

- 3-4 medium beets, about 1 lb (red or golden)
- 1 cup white vinegar
- 1/2 cup water
- 1/2 cup granulated sugar
- 1/2 tsp salt
- 1/4 tsp whole black peppercorns
- 1/4 tsp whole cloves
- 1/4 tsp mustard seeds (optional)
- 1 bay leaf (optional)

Instructions:

1. **Prepare the Beets:**
    - Wash the beets thoroughly under cold water to remove any dirt. Trim off the tops and roots. Leave the skin on to help retain color during cooking.
2. **Cook the Beets:**
    - Place the beets in a large pot and cover with water. Bring to a boil over medium-high heat, then reduce the heat to low and simmer for 30-45 minutes, or until the beets are tender when pierced with a fork.
    - Drain the beets and let them cool until they can be handled. Peel off the skins (they should easily slip off), and slice the beets into thin rounds or wedges.
3. **Prepare the Pickling Liquid:**
    - In a medium saucepan, combine the vinegar, water, sugar, salt, peppercorns, cloves, mustard seeds (if using), and bay leaf (if using). Bring to a boil over medium-high heat, stirring occasionally until the sugar and salt dissolve.
4. **Pickling Process:**
    - Add the sliced beets to the boiling pickling liquid. Reduce the heat to low and simmer for about 5 minutes.
    - Remove the saucepan from heat and let the beets cool in the pickling liquid.
5. **Storage:**
    - Transfer the pickled beets along with the pickling liquid to clean, airtight containers or jars. Make sure the beets are completely submerged in the liquid. Seal tightly.
6. **Chill and Serve:**
    - Refrigerate the pickled beets for at least 24 hours before serving to allow the flavors to develop. They will keep in the refrigerator for up to 2 weeks.

Tips:

- **Variations:** You can customize your pickled beets by adding other spices like cinnamon sticks, ginger, or red pepper flakes for a bit of heat.
- **Usage:** Pickled beets are great on their own as a side dish or snack, as part of a salad, or even in sandwiches and wraps.
- **Nutritional Benefits:** Beets are nutritious and packed with vitamins, minerals, and fiber. Pickling preserves many of these nutrients.

Homemade pickled beets are a delightful addition to your pantry, offering a burst of flavor and vibrant color to various dishes. Enjoy experimenting with different spice combinations to suit your taste preferences!

Apple Dumplings

Ingredients:

For the Dumplings:

- 2 large apples (such as Granny Smith), peeled and cored
- 1 package (2 sheets) of store-bought puff pastry or homemade pie dough

For the Filling:

- 1/4 cup granulated sugar
- 1/4 cup brown sugar
- 1 tsp ground cinnamon
- 1/4 tsp ground nutmeg
- 2 tbsp unsalted butter, cut into small pieces

For the Sauce:

- 1 cup water
- 1/2 cup granulated sugar
- 1/4 cup unsalted butter
- 1/2 tsp vanilla extract

Instructions:

1. **Prepare the Apples:**
   - Preheat your oven to 375°F (190°C).
   - Peel and core the apples. Cut each apple into quarters (you should have 8 apple quarters in total).
2. **Prepare the Filling:**
   - In a small bowl, mix together the granulated sugar, brown sugar, cinnamon, and nutmeg.
3. **Assemble the Dumplings:**
   - Roll out the puff pastry or pie dough on a lightly floured surface. Cut each sheet into 4 squares.
   - Place an apple quarter in the center of each pastry square. Sprinkle each apple with a spoonful of the sugar-spice mixture. Place a small piece of butter on top of each apple.
4. **Fold and Seal:**
   - Fold the corners of each pastry square up and over the apple, overlapping the edges to seal. Press firmly to secure the dough around the apple.
5. **Bake the Dumplings:**
   - Place the dumplings in a baking dish, seam side down. You can use a 9x13-inch baking dish or a similar size that fits all the dumplings snugly.

- Bake in the preheated oven for 30-35 minutes, or until the pastry is golden brown and crispy.

6. **Make the Sauce:**
    - While the dumplings are baking, prepare the sauce. In a small saucepan, combine the water, granulated sugar, butter, and vanilla extract. Bring to a boil over medium-high heat, stirring occasionally.

7. **Serve:**
    - Remove the baked apple dumplings from the oven. Spoon the warm sauce over the dumplings while they are still hot.

8. **Enjoy:**
    - Serve the apple dumplings warm, optionally with a scoop of vanilla ice cream or a dollop of whipped cream.

Tips:

- **Variations:** You can customize the filling by adding chopped nuts (such as pecans or walnuts) or dried fruits (like raisins or cranberries) to the sugar-spice mixture.
- **Pastry Options:** While puff pastry or pie dough is common, you can also make a simple biscuit dough or use crescent roll dough for a quicker version.
- **Storage:** Apple dumplings are best enjoyed fresh, but any leftovers can be stored in an airtight container in the refrigerator and reheated in the oven before serving.

These apple dumplings are a delightful treat, perfect for fall or any time you crave a comforting dessert. They combine the sweet and tart flavors of apples with a buttery, flaky crust and a warm, sweet sauce—truly a classic and comforting dessert!

Beef and Noodles

Ingredients:

- 1 lb beef stew meat, cubed (you can also use chuck roast or sirloin, cut into cubes)
- Salt and pepper, to taste
- 2 tbsp vegetable oil
- 1 onion, diced
- 2 cloves garlic, minced
- 2 cups beef broth
- 1 cup water
- 1 tbsp Worcestershire sauce
- 1 tsp soy sauce (optional)
- 1 tsp dried thyme (or 1 tbsp fresh thyme leaves)
- 1 bay leaf
- 8 oz egg noodles (wide or medium)
- 1/2 cup sour cream (optional, for a creamy sauce)
- Chopped fresh parsley, for garnish

Instructions:

1. **Brown the Beef:**
   - Season the beef cubes with salt and pepper. Heat the vegetable oil in a large skillet or Dutch oven over medium-high heat. Add the beef cubes in batches and brown them on all sides. Remove the browned beef to a plate and set aside.
2. **Saute the Vegetables:**
   - In the same skillet or Dutch oven, add the diced onion. Cook for 3-4 minutes until softened and translucent. Add the minced garlic and cook for another 1-2 minutes until fragrant.
3. **Deglaze the Pan:**
   - Pour in the beef broth and water, scraping up any browned bits from the bottom of the pan (this adds flavor). Stir in the Worcestershire sauce, soy sauce (if using), dried thyme, and bay leaf.
4. **Simmer the Beef:**
   - Return the browned beef cubes (and any accumulated juices) back to the skillet or Dutch oven. Bring the mixture to a simmer, then reduce the heat to low. Cover and simmer gently for 1.5 to 2 hours, or until the beef is tender and cooked through.
5. **Cook the Noodles:**
   - In a separate pot, cook the egg noodles according to the package instructions until al dente. Drain and set aside.
6. **Finish the Dish:**
   - Once the beef is tender, remove the bay leaf from the skillet or Dutch oven. If you prefer a creamy sauce, stir in the sour cream until well combined.

- Add the cooked egg noodles to the beef mixture and toss gently to coat the noodles with the sauce.
7. **Serve:**
    - Garnish with chopped fresh parsley and serve hot.

Tips:

- **Variations:** You can add vegetables such as carrots, peas, or mushrooms to the dish for added flavor and nutrition.
- **Storage:** Beef and noodles can be stored in an airtight container in the refrigerator for 3-4 days. Reheat gently on the stovetop or in the microwave before serving.
- **Serve with:** This dish pairs well with a side of steamed vegetables, a green salad, or crusty bread to soak up the sauce.

Beef and noodles is a comforting and satisfying meal that is perfect for cooler weather or any time you crave a hearty dish. Enjoy this homemade version with its tender beef and flavorful sauce!

Amish Cinnamon Bread

Ingredients:

For the Bread:

- 1 cup unsalted butter, softened
- 2 cups granulated sugar
- 2 large eggs
- 4 cups all-purpose flour
- 2 tsp baking soda
- 2 cups buttermilk (or 2 cups milk + 2 tbsp vinegar or lemon juice, let sit for 5 minutes)

For the Cinnamon-Sugar Mixture:

- 2/3 cup granulated sugar
- 2 tbsp ground cinnamon

For the Topping (optional):

- 2 tbsp unsalted butter, melted
- 2 tbsp granulated sugar
- 1/2 tsp ground cinnamon

Instructions:

1. **Preheat and Prepare:**
   - Preheat your oven to 350°F (175°C). Grease two 9x5-inch loaf pans or line them with parchment paper.
2. **Make the Cinnamon-Sugar Mixture:**
   - In a small bowl, mix together 2/3 cup sugar and 2 tablespoons of ground cinnamon. Set aside.
3. **Prepare the Bread Batter:**
   - In a large mixing bowl, cream together the softened butter and 2 cups of sugar until light and fluffy.
   - Add the eggs one at a time, beating well after each addition.
4. **Combine Dry Ingredients:**
   - In a separate bowl, whisk together the flour and baking soda.
5. **Alternating Addition:**
   - Gradually add the flour mixture to the creamed butter and sugar mixture, alternating with the buttermilk (or milk + vinegar/lemon juice mixture), beginning and ending with the flour mixture. Mix until just combined.
6. **Layering in the Loaf Pans:**
   - Pour a quarter of the batter into each of the prepared loaf pans. Sprinkle with a generous layer of the cinnamon-sugar mixture (about half of the mixture).

- Repeat with another layer of batter and cinnamon-sugar mixture. Top with the remaining batter.
7. **Optional Topping:**
   - If desired, mix together the melted butter, sugar, and cinnamon for the topping. Drizzle evenly over the top of each loaf.
8. **Bake:**
   - Bake in the preheated oven for 45-50 minutes, or until a toothpick inserted into the center comes out clean or with a few moist crumbs.
9. **Cool and Serve:**
   - Allow the loaves to cool in the pans for about 10 minutes, then remove them from the pans and transfer to a wire rack to cool completely.

Tips:

- **Variations:** You can add chopped nuts (such as pecans or walnuts) or raisins to the batter for added texture and flavor.
- **Storage:** Wrap the cooled loaves tightly in plastic wrap or store them in an airtight container. They will keep at room temperature for a few days or can be frozen for longer storage.
- **Sharing:** Amish Cinnamon Bread is often shared as a gift with friends and neighbors. Consider making extra loaves to give away!

This Amish Cinnamon Bread recipe yields moist and delicious loaves with a wonderful cinnamon swirl. It's perfect for breakfast, brunch, or as a delightful snack any time of day. Enjoy!

Hamburger Casserole

Ingredients:

- 1 lb ground beef
- 1 small onion, chopped
- 2 cloves garlic, minced
- 1 bell pepper, chopped (optional)
- 1 can (14.5 oz) diced tomatoes, drained
- 1 can (8 oz) tomato sauce
- 1 cup frozen corn (or mixed vegetables of your choice)
- 1 cup shredded cheddar cheese (or cheese of your choice)
- 2 cups cooked pasta (such as macaroni or penne) or cooked rice
- 1 tsp dried oregano
- 1 tsp dried basil
- Salt and pepper, to taste
- Fresh parsley, chopped (for garnish, optional)

Instructions:

1. **Preheat Oven:** Preheat your oven to 350°F (175°C). Grease a 9x13-inch baking dish or similar size with non-stick cooking spray.
2. **Brown the Ground Beef:** In a large skillet or frying pan, brown the ground beef over medium-high heat until fully cooked. Drain any excess fat.
3. **Saute Vegetables:** Add chopped onion, minced garlic, and bell pepper (if using) to the skillet with the cooked ground beef. Cook for 3-4 minutes until the vegetables are softened.
4. **Combine Ingredients:** Stir in the drained diced tomatoes, tomato sauce, frozen corn (or mixed vegetables), cooked pasta or rice, dried oregano, dried basil, salt, and pepper. Mix everything together until well combined.
5. **Transfer to Baking Dish:** Pour the mixture into the prepared baking dish and spread it out evenly.
6. **Top with Cheese:** Sprinkle shredded cheese evenly over the top of the casserole.
7. **Bake:** Cover the baking dish with foil and bake in the preheated oven for 25-30 minutes, or until the casserole is heated through and the cheese is melted and bubbly.
8. **Serve:** Remove from the oven and let it cool for a few minutes. Garnish with chopped fresh parsley, if desired, before serving.

Tips:

- **Variations:** Feel free to customize the casserole by adding your favorite vegetables or using different types of cheese.
- **Make-Ahead:** You can assemble the casserole ahead of time and refrigerate it, covered, until ready to bake. Add a few extra minutes to the baking time if baking from chilled.

- **Storage:** Leftovers can be stored in an airtight container in the refrigerator for 3-4 days. Reheat in the microwave or oven until warmed through.

This hamburger casserole is a family-friendly dish that's easy to make and perfect for busy weeknights. It combines hearty flavors and textures into a comforting one-dish meal that everyone will enjoy!

Whoopie Pies

Ingredients:

For the Cookies:

- 2 cups all-purpose flour
- 1/2 cup unsweetened cocoa powder
- 1 tsp baking powder
- 1/2 tsp baking soda
- 1/2 tsp salt
- 1/2 cup unsalted butter, softened
- 1 cup granulated sugar
- 1 large egg
- 1 tsp vanilla extract
- 1 cup buttermilk

For the Filling:

- 1/2 cup unsalted butter, softened
- 1 cup powdered sugar
- 1 cup marshmallow fluff (or marshmallow cream)
- 1 tsp vanilla extract

Instructions:

1. **Preheat Oven:** Preheat your oven to 350°F (175°C). Line baking sheets with parchment paper or silicone baking mats.
2. **Make the Cookies:**
    - In a medium bowl, whisk together the flour, cocoa powder, baking powder, baking soda, and salt.
3. **Cream Butter and Sugar:**
    - In a large bowl or the bowl of a stand mixer, cream together the softened butter and granulated sugar until light and fluffy.
4. **Add Egg and Vanilla:**
    - Add the egg and vanilla extract to the butter-sugar mixture. Beat until well combined.
5. **Combine Wet and Dry Ingredients:**
    - Gradually add the flour mixture to the butter mixture, alternating with the buttermilk, beginning and ending with the flour mixture. Mix until just combined.
6. **Scoop and Bake:**
    - Drop rounded tablespoons of batter onto the prepared baking sheets, spacing them about 2 inches apart.
    - Bake in the preheated oven for 10-12 minutes, or until the cookies are set and spring back lightly when touched. Remove from the oven and let cool on the

baking sheets for a few minutes before transferring to wire racks to cool completely.
7. **Make the Filling:**
    - In a medium bowl, beat together the softened butter, powdered sugar, marshmallow fluff, and vanilla extract until smooth and creamy.
8. **Assemble the Whoopie Pies:**
    - Once the cookies are completely cooled, spread a generous amount of filling on the flat side of half of the cookies.
    - Top each filled cookie with another cookie, flat side down, to create sandwich pies.
9. **Serve and Enjoy:**
    - Serve the whoopie pies immediately, or store them in an airtight container in the refrigerator until ready to serve.

Tips:

- **Variations:** You can customize whoopie pies by adding mini chocolate chips or chopped nuts to the cookie batter, or by using different flavors of filling such as peanut butter or cream cheese.
- **Storage:** Whoopie pies can be stored in the refrigerator for up to 3 days. Let them come to room temperature for about 15 minutes before serving for the best texture.

These homemade whoopie pies are soft, chocolatey, and filled with a creamy marshmallow filling—a nostalgic and delightful treat for any occasion!

Amish White Bread

Ingredients:

- 2 cups warm water (around 110°F or 45°C)
- 1/2 cup granulated sugar
- 1 1/2 tbsp active dry yeast
- 1 1/2 tsp salt
- 1/4 cup vegetable oil or melted butter
- 5-6 cups all-purpose flour

Instructions:

1. **Activate the Yeast:**
   - In a large mixing bowl or the bowl of a stand mixer, combine the warm water and sugar. Stir until the sugar is dissolved. Sprinkle the yeast over the water and let it sit for about 5-10 minutes, or until foamy.
2. **Mix the Dough:**
   - Add the salt, vegetable oil or melted butter, and 4 cups of flour to the yeast mixture. Mix with a wooden spoon or the paddle attachment of your stand mixer until smooth.
3. **Knead the Dough:**
   - Gradually add more flour, 1/2 cup at a time, until the dough begins to pull away from the sides of the bowl. You may not need to use all 6 cups of flour; stop adding flour when the dough is smooth and slightly tacky but not sticky.
   - Turn the dough out onto a lightly floured surface and knead for about 5-7 minutes, or knead with the dough hook attachment of your stand mixer on medium speed for about 5 minutes.
4. **First Rise:**
   - Place the dough in a greased bowl, turning once to coat the dough. Cover loosely with a clean kitchen towel or plastic wrap. Let the dough rise in a warm, draft-free place for about 1 hour, or until doubled in size.
5. **Shape the Loaves:**
   - Punch down the risen dough and divide it in half. Shape each half into a loaf and place into greased 9x5-inch loaf pans.
6. **Second Rise:**
   - Cover the loaf pans loosely with a clean kitchen towel or plastic wrap and let the dough rise for another 30-45 minutes, or until the dough rises just above the rim of the pans.
7. **Preheat Oven:**
   - Meanwhile, preheat your oven to 350°F (175°C).
8. **Bake the Bread:**
   - Bake the loaves in the preheated oven for 25-30 minutes, or until the tops are golden brown and the loaves sound hollow when tapped on the bottom.

- If the tops brown too quickly, you can loosely tent them with foil during the last 10 minutes of baking.
9. **Cool and Serve:**
    - Remove the bread from the pans and transfer to wire racks to cool completely before slicing.

Tips:

- **Testing for Doneness:** If you have a kitchen thermometer, the internal temperature of the bread should reach about 190-200°F (88-93°C) when fully baked.
- **Storing:** Once cooled, store Amish White Bread in an airtight container or resealable bag at room temperature for up to 3-4 days. For longer storage, wrap tightly in plastic wrap and foil, or in a freezer-safe bag, and freeze for up to 2-3 months.
- **Variations:** For a richer flavor, you can replace some of the water with milk. You can also brush the tops of the loaves with melted butter after baking for a softer crust.

Enjoy your homemade Amish White Bread sliced fresh for sandwiches, toast, or simply with butter—it's sure to be a hit at the table!

Corn Fritters

Ingredients:

- 1 cup all-purpose flour
- 1 tsp baking powder
- 1/2 tsp salt
- 1/4 tsp black pepper
- 2 large eggs
- 1/4 cup milk
- 1 tbsp melted butter or vegetable oil
- 2 cups fresh or frozen corn kernels (thawed if using frozen)
- 1/2 cup chopped green onions (optional)
- Vegetable oil, for frying

Instructions:

1. **Prepare the Batter:**
   - In a large bowl, whisk together the flour, baking powder, salt, and black pepper.
2. **Add Wet Ingredients:**
   - In another bowl, whisk together the eggs, milk, and melted butter or oil.
3. **Combine and Mix:**
   - Pour the wet ingredients into the dry ingredients and stir until just combined. The batter should be thick but still pourable.
4. **Add Corn and Green Onions:**
   - Gently fold in the corn kernels and chopped green onions (if using) until evenly distributed in the batter.
5. **Heat Oil for Frying:**
   - Heat about 1/4 inch of vegetable oil in a large skillet over medium heat until hot but not smoking. You can test if the oil is hot enough by dropping a small amount of batter into the oil; it should sizzle and start to fry immediately.
6. **Fry the Fritters:**
   - Drop spoonfuls of batter (about 2 tablespoons each) into the hot oil, spacing them a few inches apart. Flatten slightly with the back of the spoon.
7. **Cook Until Golden Brown:**
   - Fry the fritters for 2-3 minutes on each side, or until they are golden brown and crispy. Flip carefully using a spatula.
8. **Drain and Serve:**
   - Remove the cooked fritters from the oil and place them on a plate lined with paper towels to drain excess oil.
9. **Serve Warm:**
   - Serve the corn fritters warm, optionally with a dipping sauce like sour cream, salsa, or a spicy aioli.

Tips:

- **Variations:** You can add chopped herbs like cilantro or parsley, diced jalapeños for a spicy kick, or grated cheese to the batter for extra flavor.
- **Make Ahead:** Corn fritters are best served fresh and hot. However, you can prepare the batter ahead of time and fry them just before serving.
- **Storage:** Leftover corn fritters can be stored in an airtight container in the refrigerator for up to 2 days. Reheat them in a toaster oven or conventional oven to crisp them up again.

These corn fritters are crispy on the outside, tender on the inside, and bursting with sweet corn flavor—a delightful treat that's sure to please!

Dutch Meatloaf

Ingredients:

- 1 lb ground beef (or a mixture of ground beef and pork)
- 1 cup fresh breadcrumbs (from about 2 slices of bread)
- 1/2 cup milk
- 1 small onion, finely chopped
- 1 clove garlic, minced
- 1/4 cup chopped fresh parsley
- 1/4 cup grated Gouda cheese (or other mild cheese of your choice)
- 1 egg, lightly beaten
- 1 tbsp Dijon mustard
- 1 tbsp Worcestershire sauce
- Salt and pepper, to taste
- 4 slices bacon (optional, for topping)

Glaze (optional):

- 1/4 cup ketchup
- 1 tbsp brown sugar
- 1 tbsp Dijon mustard

Instructions:

1. **Preheat Oven:** Preheat your oven to 350°F (175°C). Grease a loaf pan with butter or cooking spray.
2. **Prepare Breadcrumbs:** In a small bowl, soak the fresh breadcrumbs in milk until softened.
3. **Mix Meatloaf Mixture:**
   - In a large mixing bowl, combine the ground beef, soaked breadcrumbs, chopped onion, minced garlic, chopped parsley, grated cheese, beaten egg, Dijon mustard, Worcestershire sauce, salt, and pepper. Mix well using your hands or a spoon until all ingredients are evenly combined.
4. **Shape the Meatloaf:**
   - Transfer the meat mixture to the prepared loaf pan and shape it into a loaf shape, pressing gently to compact it.
5. **Optional Glaze:**
   - In a small bowl, mix together the ketchup, brown sugar, and Dijon mustard. Spread this glaze evenly over the top of the meatloaf.
6. **Bake:**
   - If using, lay the bacon slices over the top of the meatloaf.

- Bake in the preheated oven for 1 hour to 1 hour and 15 minutes, or until the meatloaf is cooked through and the internal temperature reaches 160°F (71°C) on an instant-read thermometer.
7. **Rest and Serve:**
    - Remove the meatloaf from the oven and let it rest in the pan for 10 minutes before slicing.
8. **Serve:** Slice the Dutch meatloaf and serve warm, optionally with mashed potatoes and steamed vegetables on the side.

Tips:

- **Bacon Variation:** Adding bacon slices on top of the meatloaf not only adds flavor but also keeps the meatloaf moist during baking.
- **Cheese Options:** Besides Gouda, you can use other cheeses like Edam, Cheddar, or a blend of cheeses for different flavors.
- **Leftovers:** Leftover Dutch meatloaf can be stored in an airtight container in the refrigerator for up to 3-4 days. Reheat slices gently in the microwave or oven before serving.

This Dutch meatloaf recipe yields a moist and flavorful loaf with a hint of cheese and herbs, making it a comforting and satisfying meal for any occasion.

Amish Baked Oatmeal

Ingredients:

- 2 cups old-fashioned oats
- 1/2 cup brown sugar (or maple syrup/honey for sweetness)
- 1 tsp baking powder
- 1/2 tsp salt
- 1 tsp ground cinnamon
- 2 large eggs
- 1 1/2 cups milk (dairy or plant-based)
- 1/4 cup melted butter (or coconut oil)
- 1 tsp vanilla extract
- 1 cup fresh or frozen berries (blueberries, raspberries, or strawberries)
- 1/2 cup chopped nuts (optional, such as walnuts or pecans)

Instructions:

1. **Preheat Oven:** Preheat your oven to 350°F (175°C). Grease a 9x9-inch baking dish or similar size with butter or cooking spray.
2. **Mix Dry Ingredients:** In a large bowl, combine the oats, brown sugar (or preferred sweetener), baking powder, salt, and ground cinnamon.
3. **Add Wet Ingredients:** In another bowl, whisk together the eggs, milk, melted butter (or coconut oil), and vanilla extract.
4. **Combine Wet and Dry Ingredients:** Pour the wet ingredients into the bowl with the dry ingredients. Stir until well combined.
5. **Add Fruits and Nuts:** Gently fold in the berries and chopped nuts (if using) into the oat mixture.
6. **Bake:** Pour the oatmeal mixture into the prepared baking dish, spreading it out evenly.
7. **Bake in the Oven:** Bake for 35-40 minutes, or until the top is golden brown and the oatmeal is set.
8. **Serve:** Remove from the oven and let it cool for a few minutes before slicing. Serve warm, optionally with a drizzle of milk or yogurt on top.

Tips:

- **Variations:** You can customize Amish Baked Oatmeal by adding different fruits like sliced bananas, apples, or peaches. You can also add a sprinkle of coconut flakes or chocolate chips for added flavor.
- **Make-Ahead:** This dish can be prepared the night before and stored covered in the refrigerator. Bake it in the morning for a quick breakfast.
- **Storage:** Leftovers can be stored in an airtight container in the refrigerator for up to 4 days. Reheat individual portions in the microwave or oven before serving.

Amish Baked Oatmeal is a wholesome and satisfying breakfast that's not only delicious but also easy to prepare. It's sure to become a favorite in your breakfast rotation!

Lemon Sponge Pie

Ingredients:

For the Pie Crust:

- 1 9-inch pie crust, homemade or store-bought (pre-baked according to package instructions)

For the Lemon Filling:

- 1 cup granulated sugar
- 3 tbsp all-purpose flour
- 1/4 tsp salt
- 3 large eggs, separated
- 1 cup milk (whole milk or 2%)
- 1/4 cup fresh lemon juice (about 2-3 lemons)
- 1 tsp lemon zest
- 1 tbsp unsalted butter, melted

Instructions:

1. **Preheat Oven:** Preheat your oven to 350°F (175°C). Place the pre-baked pie crust in a 9-inch pie dish on a baking sheet for easy handling.
2. **Separate Eggs:** Separate the egg yolks from the whites into separate bowls. Set aside.
3. **Make the Lemon Filling:**
   - In a medium bowl, whisk together the sugar, flour, and salt.
   - In a separate bowl, whisk together the egg yolks, milk, lemon juice, lemon zest, and melted butter until well combined.
   - Gradually add the wet ingredients to the dry ingredients, whisking until smooth.
4. **Whip Egg Whites:**
   - In a clean bowl, using an electric mixer or stand mixer with a whisk attachment, beat the egg whites until stiff peaks form.
5. **Fold in Egg Whites:**
   - Gently fold the beaten egg whites into the lemon mixture until just combined. Be careful not to deflate the egg whites too much, as they provide the light, airy texture to the pie.
6. **Assemble and Bake:**
   - Pour the lemon filling into the pre-baked pie crust, spreading it evenly.
7. **Bake the Pie:**
   - Bake in the preheated oven for 35-40 minutes, or until the top is lightly golden brown and the filling is set. The center should jiggle slightly when gently shaken.
8. **Cool and Serve:**
   - Remove the pie from the oven and let it cool completely on a wire rack before serving. Optionally, dust with powdered sugar or serve with whipped cream.

Tips:

- **Pie Crust:** For a homemade pie crust, you can use your favorite recipe or a store-bought crust that you pre-bake according to package instructions.
- **Lemon Zest:** The lemon zest adds extra flavor and fragrance to the pie filling. Use a microplane or fine grater to zest the lemons, avoiding the bitter white pith.
- **Storage:** Store leftover Lemon Sponge Pie in the refrigerator, covered, for up to 3 days. Serve chilled or at room temperature.

This Lemon Sponge Pie recipe yields a refreshing and light dessert with a tangy lemon flavor and a fluffy texture that's sure to please any lemon lover! Enjoy it as a delightful ending to any meal or as a special treat for gatherings.

Chicken and Biscuits

Ingredients:

For the Chicken Stew:

- 1 lb boneless, skinless chicken breasts or thighs, cut into bite-sized pieces
- 2 tbsp olive oil
- 1 medium onion, chopped
- 2 cloves garlic, minced
- 2 carrots, peeled and diced
- 2 celery ribs, diced
- 1 tsp dried thyme
- 1/2 tsp dried sage
- Salt and pepper, to taste
- 1/4 cup all-purpose flour
- 3 cups chicken broth
- 1 cup frozen peas (optional)
- 1/2 cup heavy cream or half-and-half

For the Biscuit Topping:

- 2 cups all-purpose flour
- 1 tbsp baking powder
- 1/2 tsp baking soda
- 1/2 tsp salt
- 1/2 cup cold unsalted butter, cut into cubes
- 3/4 cup buttermilk (or milk)

Additional:

- Fresh parsley, chopped (for garnish, optional)

Instructions:

1. **Preheat Oven:** Preheat your oven to 400°F (200°C).
2. **Cook the Chicken Stew:**
   - In a large skillet or Dutch oven, heat olive oil over medium heat. Add the chopped onion and cook until softened, about 5 minutes.
   - Add the minced garlic, diced carrots, and diced celery. Cook for another 3-4 minutes until vegetables are slightly tender.
   - Season with dried thyme, dried sage, salt, and pepper.
   - Push the vegetables to the side of the pan and add the chicken pieces. Cook until chicken is browned on all sides, about 5-7 minutes.

- Sprinkle flour over the chicken and vegetables. Stir well to coat everything evenly with the flour.
- Gradually pour in the chicken broth, stirring constantly to prevent lumps. Bring to a simmer and cook until the sauce thickens, about 5-7 minutes.
- Stir in the frozen peas (if using) and heavy cream. Remove from heat and set aside.

3. **Make the Biscuit Dough:**
    - In a large bowl, whisk together the flour, baking powder, baking soda, and salt.
    - Add the cold cubed butter to the flour mixture. Using a pastry cutter or your fingers, work the butter into the flour until it resembles coarse crumbs.
    - Gradually pour in the buttermilk, stirring with a fork until the dough just comes together.

4. **Assemble and Bake:**
    - Transfer the chicken stew mixture into a 9x13-inch baking dish or a large oven-safe skillet.
    - Drop spoonfuls of the biscuit dough over the top of the chicken stew, evenly covering the surface.

5. **Bake the Dish:**
    - Place the baking dish in the preheated oven and bake for 25-30 minutes, or until the biscuits are golden brown and cooked through.

6. **Serve:** Remove from the oven and let it cool for a few minutes. Garnish with chopped fresh parsley, if desired, and serve warm.

Tips:

- **Vegetables:** Feel free to add other vegetables such as diced potatoes or bell peppers to the chicken stew for added flavor and texture.
- **Make-Ahead:** You can prepare the chicken stew ahead of time and assemble with the biscuit topping just before baking.
- **Storage:** Leftovers can be stored in an airtight container in the refrigerator for up to 3-4 days. Reheat in the oven or microwave until warmed through.

This chicken and biscuits recipe is a satisfying meal that's perfect for a cozy dinner with family or a comforting dish to share with friends. Enjoy the creamy chicken stew with fluffy biscuits for a delicious homemade meal!

Amish Peanut Butter Pie

Ingredients:

For the Pie Crust:

- 1 1/2 cups graham cracker crumbs
- 1/4 cup granulated sugar
- 6 tbsp unsalted butter, melted

For the Peanut Butter Filling:

- 1 cup creamy peanut butter
- 8 oz (1 package) cream cheese, softened
- 1 cup powdered sugar
- 1 tsp vanilla extract
- 1 cup heavy cream, whipped to stiff peaks

For Garnish (optional):

- Chocolate shavings or chopped peanuts

Instructions:

1. **Prepare the Pie Crust:**
   - In a medium bowl, combine the graham cracker crumbs, granulated sugar, and melted butter. Mix until well combined and the mixture resembles wet sand.
   - Press the mixture evenly into the bottom and up the sides of a 9-inch pie dish. Use the back of a spoon or a flat-bottomed measuring cup to press it firmly.
   - Refrigerate the crust while preparing the filling.
2. **Make the Peanut Butter Filling:**
   - In a large mixing bowl, beat together the creamy peanut butter and softened cream cheese until smooth and well combined.
   - Add the powdered sugar and vanilla extract, and continue to beat until smooth.
3. **Fold in Whipped Cream:**
   - Gently fold the whipped cream into the peanut butter mixture until evenly incorporated. Be careful not to deflate the whipped cream too much, as it adds lightness to the filling.
4. **Assemble the Pie:**
   - Spoon the peanut butter filling into the prepared graham cracker crust, smoothing the top with a spatula.
5. **Chill the Pie:**
   - Refrigerate the pie for at least 4 hours, or preferably overnight, until the filling is firm and set.
6. **Garnish and Serve:**

- Before serving, garnish the pie with chocolate shavings or chopped peanuts for added texture and flavor.
7. **Slice and Enjoy:**
    - Slice the chilled Amish Peanut Butter Pie and serve cold. Enjoy the creamy, peanut buttery goodness!

Tips:

- **Variations:** For a chocolate twist, you can add a layer of chocolate ganache on top of the graham cracker crust before adding the peanut butter filling.
- **Storage:** Keep leftover pie covered in the refrigerator for up to 3-4 days. The crust may soften slightly over time, but the flavors will still be delicious.

This Amish Peanut Butter Pie is a decadent treat that's perfect for any occasion, from family gatherings to potluck dinners. It's sure to satisfy any peanut butter lover's cravings with its creamy texture and rich flavor!

Church Spread

Ingredients:

- 1 cup granulated sugar
- 1 cup evaporated milk
- 1/2 cup unsalted butter
- 1 tsp vanilla extract

Instructions:

1. **Combine Ingredients:**
   - In a medium saucepan, combine the granulated sugar, evaporated milk, and unsalted butter.
2. **Cook Over Medium Heat:**
   - Cook the mixture over medium heat, stirring constantly, until the butter is melted and the sugar is dissolved.
3. **Simmer and Thicken:**
   - Bring the mixture to a gentle boil, then reduce the heat to low. Let it simmer for about 5-7 minutes, stirring occasionally, until it thickens slightly.
4. **Remove from Heat:**
   - Remove the saucepan from the heat and stir in the vanilla extract. Allow the Church Spread to cool completely before using it in recipes.

Notes:

- **Usage:** Church Spread can be used as a filling for pies (such as Church Spread pie), as a topping for cakes or desserts, or even spread on bread or biscuits.
- **Storage:** Store any leftover Church Spread in an airtight container in the refrigerator. It should keep well for about 1 week.

This simple Church Spread recipe captures the essence of traditional Amish and Mennonite cooking, offering a sweet and creamy addition to various homemade desserts and treats.

Amish Egg Noodles

Ingredients:

- 2 cups all-purpose flour
- 1/2 tsp salt
- 2 large eggs
- 1/4 cup water (more as needed)
- Extra flour for dusting

Instructions:

1. **Prepare the Dough:**
   - In a large mixing bowl, combine the flour and salt. Make a well in the center of the flour mixture.
2. **Add Eggs and Water:**
   - Crack the eggs into the well. Using a fork, gently beat the eggs while gradually incorporating the flour from the sides of the well.
3. **Form the Dough:**
   - As the mixture starts to come together, gradually add the water, a tablespoon at a time, until a dough forms. You may not need to use all of the water.
   - Use your hands to knead the dough in the bowl or on a lightly floured surface until smooth and elastic, about 5-7 minutes.
4. **Rest the Dough:**
   - Cover the dough with a clean kitchen towel or plastic wrap and let it rest for at least 15-20 minutes at room temperature. This allows the gluten to relax and makes rolling easier.
5. **Roll Out the Noodles:**
   - Divide the dough into 2-3 portions. On a lightly floured surface, roll out each portion of dough with a rolling pin until very thin, about 1/16 inch thick or even thinner if possible.
   - Alternatively, you can use a pasta machine to roll out the dough into thin sheets.
6. **Cut the Noodles:**
   - Dust the rolled-out dough lightly with flour. Fold the dough over itself several times and then cut into strips of desired width using a sharp knife or a pizza cutter. Traditional Amish noodles are typically wider, about 1/4 inch wide.
7. **Dry or Cook Immediately:**
   - At this point, you can either cook the noodles immediately in boiling water or let them air dry for about an hour before storing or using them.
8. **Cook the Noodles:**
   - Bring a large pot of salted water to a boil. Add the noodles and cook until al dente, about 3-5 minutes depending on the thickness of the noodles. Stir occasionally to prevent sticking.
9. **Serve:**

- Drain the noodles and serve them as desired. They are delicious tossed with butter, herbs, or added to soups and stews.

Tips:

- **Storage:** If not using immediately, let the noodles air dry completely on a floured surface for about an hour. Once dry, store them in an airtight container or resealable bag in a cool, dry place for up to 1 week.
- **Variations:** For richer noodles, you can use more egg yolks or replace some of the water with additional eggs.
- **Cooking Time:** Cooking time may vary depending on the thickness of the noodles. Taste test for desired texture.

Homemade Amish egg noodles are a wonderful way to enjoy the comfort of fresh pasta in various dishes. They add a hearty touch to soups or make a delicious side dish when simply buttered and seasoned.

Pennsylvania Dutch Funnel Cake

Ingredients:

- 2 cups all-purpose flour
- 1 tsp baking powder
- 1/2 tsp salt
- 2 tbsp granulated sugar
- 1 1/4 cups milk
- 2 large eggs
- 1/2 tsp vanilla extract
- Vegetable oil, for frying
- Powdered sugar, for dusting

Instructions:

1. **Prepare the Batter:**
    - In a large mixing bowl, whisk together the flour, baking powder, salt, and granulated sugar.
2. **Make the Funnel Cake Batter:**
    - In another bowl, whisk together the milk, eggs, and vanilla extract until well combined.
3. **Combine Wet and Dry Ingredients:**
    - Gradually pour the wet ingredients into the dry ingredients, whisking constantly, until a smooth batter forms. The batter should be thick but pourable. If it's too thick, add a little more milk.
4. **Heat Oil for Frying:**
    - In a large, deep skillet or pot, heat about 2 inches of vegetable oil to 375°F (190°C). Use a candy thermometer to monitor the temperature for best results.
5. **Prepare for Frying:**
    - Pour the funnel cake batter into a large squeeze bottle or a plastic bag with a corner snipped off. This will make it easier to control when pouring into the hot oil.
6. **Fry the Funnel Cakes:**
    - Hold the squeeze bottle or plastic bag over the hot oil and squeeze the batter in a circular motion, starting from the center and spiraling outward. Create a lacy pattern, making sure not to overlap too much batter.
7. **Fry Until Golden Brown:**
    - Fry each funnel cake for about 1-2 minutes on each side, or until golden brown and crispy. Use tongs or a slotted spoon to carefully flip the funnel cake halfway through frying.
8. **Drain and Serve:**
    - Remove the funnel cake from the oil and place it on a plate lined with paper towels to drain excess oil.

9. **Dust with Powdered Sugar:**
   - Generously dust the warm funnel cake with powdered sugar using a fine-mesh sieve.
10. **Serve Warm:**
    - Enjoy the Pennsylvania Dutch Funnel Cake warm and fresh. It's best served immediately after frying.

Tips:

- **Variations:** You can top the funnel cake with other toppings such as chocolate syrup, fruit preserves, whipped cream, or even ice cream for a decadent dessert.
- **Storage:** Funnel cakes are best enjoyed fresh and hot. If you have leftovers, you can reheat them in the oven at a low temperature to crisp them up again.
- **Safety Note:** Be cautious when working with hot oil. Fry the funnel cakes in batches to avoid overcrowding the pan and maintain the oil temperature.

Making Pennsylvania Dutch Funnel Cake at home is a fun and delicious way to recreate the fairground experience. It's a treat loved by all ages, perfect for special occasions or simply when you crave something sweet and crispy!

Chicken Corn Pie

Ingredients:

For the Pie Filling:

- 2 cups cooked chicken, diced or shredded
- 2 cups corn kernels (fresh, canned, or frozen)
- 1 cup chicken broth
- 1/2 cup milk or cream
- 1/4 cup unsalted butter
- 1/4 cup all-purpose flour
- 1 small onion, finely chopped
- 1 celery rib, finely chopped
- 1 carrot, finely chopped
- 1/2 tsp dried thyme
- Salt and pepper, to taste

For the Pie Crust:

- 2 store-bought or homemade pie crusts (enough for top and bottom crust)

Instructions:

1. **Prepare the Pie Crust:**
    - Preheat your oven to 375°F (190°C).
    - Roll out one of the pie crusts and line a 9-inch pie dish. Trim any excess dough and crimp the edges. Set aside.
2. **Make the Filling:**
    - In a large skillet or saucepan, melt the butter over medium heat. Add the chopped onion, celery, and carrot. Cook until vegetables are softened, about 5-7 minutes.
3. **Add Flour and Thyme:**
    - Sprinkle the flour over the vegetables and stir to combine. Cook for 1-2 minutes to cook off the raw flour taste.
4. **Create the Sauce:**
    - Gradually add the chicken broth and milk, stirring constantly to prevent lumps. Cook until the mixture thickens and comes to a simmer, about 5 minutes.
5. **Combine Chicken and Corn:**
    - Stir in the diced or shredded chicken and corn kernels. Season with dried thyme, salt, and pepper to taste. Remove from heat.
6. **Assemble and Bake:**
    - Pour the chicken and corn filling into the prepared pie crust.
7. **Top with Second Crust:**

- Roll out the second pie crust and place it over the filling. Trim any excess dough and crimp the edges to seal. Cut a few slits in the top crust to allow steam to escape.

8. **Bake the Pie:**
   - Place the pie on a baking sheet (to catch any drips) and bake in the preheated oven for 40-45 minutes, or until the crust is golden brown and the filling is bubbly.
9. **Cool and Serve:**
   - Remove from the oven and let the pie cool for 10-15 minutes before slicing and serving.

Tips:

- **Chicken:** You can use leftover cooked chicken or rotisserie chicken for convenience.
- **Vegetables:** Feel free to add other vegetables like peas or bell peppers for extra flavor and color.
- **Storage:** Leftover Chicken Corn Pie can be stored covered in the refrigerator for 3-4 days. Reheat in the oven or microwave until warmed through.

Chicken Corn Pie is a delicious and hearty dish that's perfect for a family dinner or potluck. It combines tender chicken and sweet corn in a creamy sauce, all encased in a flaky, buttery crust. Enjoy the comfort of homemade pie with this classic recipe!

Apple Slaw

Ingredients:

- 2 cups thinly sliced cabbage (green or red cabbage)
- 2 medium apples, cored and julienned (choose crisp varieties like Granny Smith or Honeycrisp)
- 1 carrot, grated or julienned
- 1/4 cup chopped fresh parsley or cilantro (optional, for garnish)

For the Dressing:

- 1/4 cup mayonnaise
- 2 tbsp apple cider vinegar
- 1 tbsp honey or maple syrup (adjust to taste)
- 1/2 tsp Dijon mustard
- Salt and pepper, to taste

Instructions:

1. **Prepare the Dressing:**
   - In a small bowl, whisk together the mayonnaise, apple cider vinegar, honey or maple syrup, Dijon mustard, salt, and pepper until smooth and well combined. Adjust sweetness and acidity to taste.
2. **Assemble the Slaw:**
   - In a large bowl, combine the thinly sliced cabbage, julienned apples, and grated carrot.
3. **Add the Dressing:**
   - Pour the dressing over the cabbage, apples, and carrot mixture. Toss gently to coat everything evenly with the dressing.
4. **Chill and Serve:**
   - Cover the bowl with plastic wrap or transfer the slaw to an airtight container. Refrigerate for at least 30 minutes to allow the flavors to meld and the slaw to chill.
5. **Garnish and Serve:**
   - Just before serving, garnish with chopped fresh parsley or cilantro, if desired. Serve chilled as a side dish or topping for sandwiches, burgers, or tacos.

Tips:

- **Variations:** Feel free to customize your apple slaw by adding additional ingredients such as sliced red onion, dried cranberries, toasted nuts (like walnuts or almonds), or shredded cheese.
- **Storage:** Apple slaw can be stored in the refrigerator for up to 2-3 days. Keep it in an airtight container to maintain freshness.

- **Crisp Apples:** Choose apples that are firm and crisp for the best texture in your slaw.

This apple slaw recipe is perfect for adding a fresh and crunchy element to your meals. It's versatile, delicious, and a great way to enjoy seasonal apples in a savory and satisfying salad.

Homemade Root Beer

Ingredients:

- 2 quarts (8 cups) water
- 1 cup sassafras root bark (or substitute with 1/4 cup sarsaparilla root and 1/4 cup wintergreen leaf as alternatives)
- 1 cup granulated sugar
- 1 cup molasses
- 1/4 tsp active dry yeast
- 1/4 cup lukewarm water (about 110°F or 45°C)
- 2 tbsp ginger root, grated (optional, for added spice)

Equipment Needed:

- Large pot
- Fine mesh strainer or cheesecloth
- Funnel
- Large pitcher or bottles for storing

Instructions:

1. **Prepare the Sassafras Mixture:**
   - In a large pot, bring 2 quarts of water to a boil. Remove the pot from heat and add the sassafras root bark (or alternative roots and leaves) and grated ginger root, if using.
   - Cover the pot and let it steep for about 30 minutes to 1 hour to extract the flavors.
2. **Strain the Mixture:**
   - After steeping, strain the liquid through a fine mesh strainer or cheesecloth into a clean bowl or another pot to remove the roots and ginger. Press on the solids to extract as much liquid as possible.
3. **Sweeten the Root Beer:**
   - Return the strained liquid to the pot. Stir in the granulated sugar and molasses until they are completely dissolved.
4. **Activate the Yeast:**
   - In a small bowl, dissolve the active dry yeast in 1/4 cup of lukewarm water. Let it sit for about 5-10 minutes until it becomes frothy.
5. **Combine and Ferment:**
   - Pour the yeast mixture into the pot with the sweetened root beer liquid. Stir gently to combine.
   - Cover the pot loosely with a clean cloth or plastic wrap and let it sit at room temperature for about 2-3 hours to allow the yeast to ferment. During this time, natural carbonation will develop.
6. **Bottle the Root Beer:**

- After fermentation, carefully pour the root beer into clean bottles using a funnel. Leave about 1 inch of headspace at the top of each bottle.

7. **Cap and Refrigerate:**
   - Tightly cap the bottles and refrigerate them for at least 24 hours before consuming. This allows the flavors to meld and the carbonation to develop further.

8. **Serve and Enjoy:**
   - Once chilled, serve your homemade root beer over ice and enjoy its unique flavor! Remember to store any unused root beer in the refrigerator.

Tips:

- **Safety Note:** Exercise caution when using active dry yeast and fermenting. Ensure your containers are clean and sanitized to avoid contamination.
- **Flavor Adjustments:** Feel free to adjust the amount of sugar, molasses, or spices to suit your taste preferences.
- **Bottling:** Use bottles that are designed to handle carbonation, such as glass soda bottles or plastic PET bottles.

Making homemade root beer is a delightful experience that results in a beverage with natural flavors and carbonation. Experiment with different herbs and spices to create your own signature root beer recipe!

Dutch Meatballs

Ingredients:

- 1/2 lb ground beef
- 1/2 lb ground pork
- 1 small onion, finely chopped
- 2 cloves garlic, minced
- 2 tbsp butter
- 3 tbsp all-purpose flour
- 1 cup beef broth
- 1/4 cup milk or cream
- 1/4 tsp ground nutmeg
- Salt and pepper, to taste
- 1/4 cup fresh parsley, finely chopped (optional, for garnish)
- Breadcrumbs (about 1 cup)
- 2 eggs, beaten
- Vegetable oil, for frying

Instructions:

1. **Cook the Meat Mixture:**
    - In a large skillet, melt the butter over medium heat. Add the chopped onion and garlic, and cook until softened and translucent, about 3-4 minutes.
2. **Add Ground Meat:**
    - Add the ground beef and ground pork to the skillet. Cook, breaking up the meat with a spoon or spatula, until browned and cooked through. Drain any excess fat if necessary.
3. **Make the Roux:**
    - Sprinkle the flour over the meat mixture and stir well to combine. Cook for 1-2 minutes to cook off the raw flour taste.
4. **Add Broth and Milk:**
    - Gradually pour in the beef broth and milk or cream, stirring constantly to prevent lumps from forming. Bring to a simmer and cook until the mixture thickens, about 5 minutes.
5. **Season and Cool:**
    - Season the mixture with ground nutmeg, salt, and pepper to taste. Remove from heat and let it cool to room temperature. The mixture will thicken as it cools.
6. **Shape the Meatballs:**
    - Once cooled, shape the meat mixture into small balls, about 1 inch in diameter. Roll each ball in breadcrumbs, then dip into beaten eggs, and roll again in breadcrumbs to coat evenly. Repeat for all meatballs.
7. **Fry the Meatballs:**

- In a large skillet or pot, heat enough vegetable oil over medium-high heat for frying (about 1-2 inches deep). Fry the meatballs in batches until golden brown and crispy, about 3-4 minutes per batch. Use a slotted spoon to transfer the fried meatballs to a plate lined with paper towels to drain excess oil.
8. **Serve:**
    - Serve the Dutch meatballs hot with mustard for dipping. Garnish with chopped fresh parsley, if desired.

Tips:

- **Variations:** Some recipes use a mixture of ground beef and veal or even chicken for lighter options.
- **Make Ahead:** You can prepare the meat mixture and shape the meatballs ahead of time. Refrigerate them until ready to fry.
- **Storage:** Leftover Dutch meatballs can be stored in an airtight container in the refrigerator for up to 3 days. Reheat them in the oven to crisp them up again.

Dutch meatballs are a delicious appetizer or snack that pairs well with a cold beer or as part of a larger Dutch-inspired meal. Enjoy their crispy exterior and savory, creamy filling!

Amish Broccoli Salad

Ingredients:

- 4 cups fresh broccoli florets (about 2 medium heads)
- 1 cup shredded cheddar cheese
- 1/2 cup red onion, finely chopped
- 1/2 cup raisins or dried cranberries (optional, for sweetness)
- 1/2 cup sunflower seeds or chopped nuts (optional, for crunch)
- 1/2 lb bacon, cooked and crumbled (optional, for added flavor)

For the Dressing:

- 1 cup mayonnaise
- 1/4 cup granulated sugar (adjust to taste)
- 2 tbsp apple cider vinegar
- Salt and pepper, to taste

Instructions:

1. **Prepare the Broccoli:**
   - Wash the broccoli florets thoroughly and trim them into bite-sized pieces. Place them in a large mixing bowl.
2. **Add Additional Ingredients:**
   - To the bowl with broccoli, add shredded cheddar cheese, finely chopped red onion, raisins or dried cranberries (if using), sunflower seeds or chopped nuts (if using), and crumbled bacon (if using).
3. **Make the Dressing:**
   - In a small bowl, whisk together the mayonnaise, granulated sugar, apple cider vinegar, salt, and pepper until smooth and well combined.
4. **Combine and Chill:**
   - Pour the dressing over the broccoli mixture. Toss gently until all ingredients are evenly coated with the dressing.
5. **Chill Before Serving:**
   - Cover the bowl with plastic wrap or transfer the salad to an airtight container. Refrigerate for at least 1 hour before serving to allow the flavors to meld together.
6. **Serve:**
   - Just before serving, give the salad a quick toss. Taste and adjust seasoning if needed. Serve cold as a side dish or light lunch.

Tips:

- **Variations:** Feel free to customize the salad by adding different ingredients like diced apples, sliced grapes, or even cooked pasta for a heartier dish.

- **Make-Ahead:** Amish broccoli salad can be made a day in advance. Keep it refrigerated until ready to serve.
- **Storage:** Leftover salad can be stored in the refrigerator for up to 2-3 days. The broccoli may soften slightly over time, but the flavors will still be delicious.

Amish broccoli salad is a refreshing and satisfying dish that's perfect for potlucks, picnics, or as a side for grilled meats. It's loved for its combination of textures and flavors, making it a favorite among many.

Zucchini Bread

Ingredients:

- 2 cups grated zucchini (about 2 medium zucchinis)
- 2 cups all-purpose flour
- 1 tsp baking powder
- 1/2 tsp baking soda
- 1/2 tsp salt
- 1 tsp ground cinnamon
- 1/4 tsp ground nutmeg
- 2 large eggs
- 1 cup granulated sugar
- 1/2 cup vegetable oil or melted butter
- 1 tsp vanilla extract
- Optional add-ins: 1/2 cup chopped nuts (walnuts or pecans), 1/2 cup raisins, or chocolate chips

Instructions:

1. **Preheat Oven and Prepare Pan:**
   - Preheat your oven to 350°F (175°C). Grease and flour a 9x5-inch loaf pan, or line it with parchment paper for easier removal.
2. **Grate the Zucchini:**
   - Grate the zucchini using a box grater or food processor. If the grated zucchini is very watery, squeeze out excess moisture using a clean kitchen towel or paper towels.
3. **Mix Dry Ingredients:**
   - In a large bowl, whisk together the flour, baking powder, baking soda, salt, cinnamon, and nutmeg until well combined.
4. **Prepare Wet Ingredients:**
   - In another bowl, whisk together the eggs, granulated sugar, vegetable oil or melted butter, and vanilla extract until smooth.
5. **Combine Wet and Dry Ingredients:**
   - Pour the wet ingredients into the bowl with the dry ingredients. Stir gently with a spatula or wooden spoon until just combined. Do not overmix.
6. **Add Zucchini and Optional Add-Ins:**
   - Fold in the grated zucchini and any optional add-ins (nuts, raisins, chocolate chips) until evenly distributed throughout the batter.
7. **Bake the Bread:**
   - Pour the batter into the prepared loaf pan, spreading it evenly. Tap the pan gently on the countertop to remove any air bubbles.
   - Bake in the preheated oven for 50-60 minutes, or until a toothpick inserted into the center comes out clean or with a few moist crumbs.

8. **Cool and Serve:**
   - Allow the zucchini bread to cool in the pan for 10-15 minutes, then transfer it to a wire rack to cool completely before slicing.

Tips:

- **Storage:** Zucchini bread can be stored at room temperature, tightly wrapped or in an airtight container, for up to 3-4 days. It can also be frozen for longer storage.
- **Variations:** For a healthier version, you can reduce the sugar and use whole wheat flour or a combination of all-purpose and whole wheat flour.
- **Serve:** Enjoy zucchini bread slices plain, toasted, or with a smear of butter or cream cheese.

Zucchini bread is a delicious treat that balances sweetness with the subtle flavor of zucchini. It's perfect for breakfast, as a snack, or even as a dessert. Enjoy the moist and tender texture along with the comforting spices!

Pork and Sauerkraut

Ingredients:

- 2 lbs pork loin or pork shoulder, trimmed and cut into chunks
- 1 lb sauerkraut, drained and rinsed (if desired, for milder flavor)
- 1 onion, chopped
- 2 cloves garlic, minced
- 1 tsp caraway seeds (optional, for additional flavor)
- 1 cup chicken broth or beer
- Salt and pepper, to taste
- 2 tbsp vegetable oil or butter
- Chopped fresh parsley, for garnish (optional)

Instructions:

1. **Preheat Oven:**
   - Preheat your oven to 325°F (160°C).
2. **Brown the Pork:**
   - In a large oven-safe pot or Dutch oven, heat vegetable oil or butter over medium-high heat. Season the pork pieces with salt and pepper. Brown the pork in batches until golden brown on all sides. Remove and set aside.
3. **Cook Onions and Garlic:**
   - Add chopped onion to the pot and cook until softened, about 3-4 minutes. Add minced garlic and caraway seeds (if using) and cook for another minute until fragrant.
4. **Combine Pork and Sauerkraut:**
   - Return the browned pork to the pot. Add the drained and rinsed sauerkraut. Stir gently to combine.
5. **Add Liquid:**
   - Pour in the chicken broth or beer, enough to almost cover the pork and sauerkraut mixture. Bring to a simmer.
6. **Bake:**
   - Cover the pot with a lid and transfer it to the preheated oven. Bake for 2 to 2 1/2 hours, or until the pork is tender and cooked through. Stir occasionally during cooking.
7. **Serve:**
   - Once done, taste and adjust seasoning with salt and pepper if needed. Serve hot, garnished with chopped fresh parsley if desired.

Tips:

- **Variations:** You can add diced apples, potatoes, or carrots to the dish for added sweetness and texture.

- **Slow Cooker Method:** Alternatively, you can cook pork and sauerkraut in a slow cooker on low for 6-8 hours, or on high for 3-4 hours.
- **Side Dishes:** Serve pork and sauerkraut with mashed potatoes, crusty bread, or a side of steamed vegetables.

Pork and sauerkraut is a hearty and satisfying dish that's perfect for a comforting dinner. The pork becomes tender and flavorful, complemented by the tangy sauerkraut and aromatic spices. Enjoy this traditional dish with family and friends!

Molasses Cookies

Ingredients:

- 2 1/4 cups all-purpose flour
- 2 tsp baking soda
- 1/2 tsp salt
- 1 tsp ground cinnamon
- 1 tsp ground ginger
- 1/2 tsp ground cloves
- 3/4 cup unsalted butter, softened
- 1 cup granulated sugar, plus extra for rolling
- 1/4 cup molasses (choose dark or robust molasses for richer flavor)
- 1 large egg
- 1 tsp vanilla extract

Instructions:

1. **Preheat Oven:**
   - Preheat your oven to 375°F (190°C). Line baking sheets with parchment paper or silicone mats.
2. **Whisk Dry Ingredients:**
   - In a medium bowl, whisk together the flour, baking soda, salt, cinnamon, ginger, and cloves until well combined. Set aside.
3. **Cream Butter and Sugar:**
   - In a large bowl or using a stand mixer fitted with the paddle attachment, cream together the softened butter and 1 cup of granulated sugar until light and fluffy, about 2-3 minutes.
4. **Add Wet Ingredients:**
   - Add the molasses, egg, and vanilla extract to the creamed butter and sugar. Beat until well combined, scraping down the sides of the bowl as needed.
5. **Combine Dry Ingredients:**
   - Gradually add the dry ingredients to the wet ingredients, mixing on low speed until just combined. Do not overmix.
6. **Chill the Dough (Optional):**
   - For easier handling and to prevent spreading, chill the cookie dough in the refrigerator for 30-60 minutes. This step is optional but recommended if the dough feels too soft.
7. **Form Cookie Dough Balls:**
   - Scoop out tablespoon-sized portions of dough and roll them into balls. Roll each ball in granulated sugar to coat evenly.
8. **Bake the Cookies:**
   - Place the cookie dough balls onto the prepared baking sheets, spacing them about 2 inches apart. Flatten slightly with the bottom of a glass or fork.

9. **Bake:**
   - Bake in the preheated oven for 9-11 minutes, or until the edges are set and tops are cracked. The cookies will still be soft in the center.
10. **Cool and Serve:**
    - Allow the cookies to cool on the baking sheets for 5 minutes, then transfer them to a wire rack to cool completely.

Tips:

- **Molasses Options:** Use dark or robust molasses for a stronger flavor, or mild molasses for a lighter taste.
- **Storage:** Store molasses cookies in an airtight container at room temperature for up to 1 week. They can also be frozen for longer storage.
- **Spice Adjustment:** Feel free to adjust the spices to your taste preferences. You can increase or decrease the amounts of cinnamon, ginger, and cloves.

These molasses cookies are sure to be a hit with their soft texture and warm, spiced flavor. They're perfect for holiday baking or any time you crave a comforting, homemade treat. Enjoy!

Chicken Salad

Ingredients:

- 2 cups cooked chicken, shredded or diced (about 2 medium chicken breasts)
- 1/2 cup celery, finely chopped
- 1/4 cup red onion, finely chopped (optional)
- 1/4 cup mayonnaise (adjust amount to your preference)
- 1 tbsp Dijon mustard (optional, for extra flavor)
- 1 tbsp fresh lemon juice
- Salt and pepper, to taste
- Optional add-ins: chopped nuts (like almonds or pecans), dried cranberries, diced apples, grapes, chopped fresh herbs (like parsley or dill)

Instructions:

1. **Cook and Prepare Chicken:**
   - Cook chicken breasts by boiling, baking, grilling, or using leftover cooked chicken. Shred or dice the chicken into bite-sized pieces.
2. **Mix Dressing:**
   - In a large bowl, whisk together mayonnaise, Dijon mustard (if using), fresh lemon juice, salt, and pepper until smooth and well combined.
3. **Combine Ingredients:**
   - Add cooked chicken, chopped celery, and red onion (if using) to the bowl with the dressing. Mix gently until all ingredients are evenly coated with the dressing.
4. **Add Optional Add-Ins:**
   - If desired, add chopped nuts, dried cranberries, diced apples, grapes, or chopped fresh herbs to the chicken salad mixture. Stir gently to combine.
5. **Chill and Serve:**
   - Cover the bowl with plastic wrap or transfer the chicken salad to an airtight container. Refrigerate for at least 30 minutes to allow the flavors to meld together.
6. **Serve:**
   - Serve chicken salad chilled as a sandwich filling, wrap filling, or on top of a bed of lettuce as a salad. It can also be enjoyed with crackers or on its own.

Tips:

- **Chicken Preparation:** You can use leftover cooked chicken, rotisserie chicken, or even canned chicken for convenience.
- **Texture:** Adjust the texture of the chicken salad by shredding or dicing the chicken to your preference.
- **Variations:** Experiment with different add-ins such as chopped avocado, diced bell peppers, or a sprinkle of curry powder for a twist on flavors.

This classic chicken salad recipe is easy to customize based on your preferences and what you have on hand. It's perfect for quick lunches, picnics, or as a light dinner option. Enjoy the creamy texture and delicious flavors of homemade chicken salad!

Amish Pot Roast

Ingredients:

- 3-4 lbs beef chuck roast
- Salt and pepper, to taste
- 2 tbsp vegetable oil or butter
- 1 onion, sliced
- 2-3 garlic cloves, minced
- 4-5 carrots, peeled and cut into chunks
- 4-5 potatoes, peeled and cut into chunks
- 1 cup beef broth
- 1/2 cup red wine or water (optional)
- 2 tbsp Worcestershire sauce
- 2 tbsp tomato paste
- 1 tbsp brown sugar (optional, for sweetness)
- 1 tsp dried thyme
- 1 tsp dried rosemary
- 1 bay leaf
- Chopped fresh parsley, for garnish (optional)

Instructions:

1. **Preheat Oven:**
   - Preheat your oven to 325°F (160°C).
2. **Season and Sear the Roast:**
   - Pat the beef chuck roast dry with paper towels and season generously with salt and pepper. Heat vegetable oil or butter in a large oven-safe pot or Dutch oven over medium-high heat. Sear the roast on all sides until browned, about 4-5 minutes per side. Remove the roast and set it aside.
3. **Saute Vegetables:**
   - In the same pot, add sliced onion and minced garlic. Cook, stirring occasionally, until onions are translucent and garlic is fragrant, about 3-4 minutes.
4. **Combine Ingredients:**
   - Return the seared roast to the pot. Add carrots, potatoes, beef broth, red wine or water (if using), Worcestershire sauce, tomato paste, brown sugar (if using), dried thyme, dried rosemary, and bay leaf. Stir to combine.
5. **Braise the Pot Roast:**
   - Cover the pot with a lid and transfer it to the preheated oven. Braise the pot roast for 3-4 hours, or until the meat is fork-tender and easily pulls apart. Check occasionally and add more broth or water if needed to keep the roast moist.
6. **Serve:**

- Once done, remove the pot roast from the oven. Discard the bay leaf. Taste and adjust seasoning if necessary. Garnish with chopped fresh parsley, if desired. Serve the pot roast with the vegetables and pan juices.

Tips:

- **Slow Cooker Method:** Alternatively, you can cook the Amish pot roast in a slow cooker on low for 8-10 hours, or on high for 4-6 hours.
- **Variations:** Feel free to customize the vegetables based on what you have available or prefer. You can also add mushrooms, celery, or parsnips.
- **Serving Suggestions:** Amish pot roast is delicious served with mashed potatoes, buttered noodles, or crusty bread to soak up the flavorful juices.

This Amish-style pot roast recipe yields tender, flavorful meat and vegetables, perfect for a comforting family meal. Enjoy the hearty flavors and aroma that fill your kitchen as it cooks!

Red Beet Eggs

Ingredients:

- 6-8 hard-boiled eggs, peeled
- 1 can (15 oz) sliced or whole beets, with juice
- 1/2 cup apple cider vinegar or white vinegar
- 1/4 cup granulated sugar
- 1/2 cup water
- 1 tsp whole black peppercorns
- 1 tsp salt

Instructions:

1. **Prepare the Brine:**
   - In a medium saucepan, combine the beet juice (from the can of beets), vinegar, sugar, water, peppercorns, and salt. Bring the mixture to a boil over medium-high heat. Stir until the sugar is dissolved. Remove from heat and let cool slightly.
2. **Layer Eggs and Beets:**
   - Place the peeled hard-boiled eggs and sliced or whole beets in a clean glass jar or container with a lid. Layer them alternately for even distribution of color and flavor.
3. **Pour the Brine:**
   - Pour the warm brine mixture over the eggs and beets in the jar, ensuring they are completely submerged. If needed, use a clean spoon to gently press down on the eggs to ensure they are covered by the brine.
4. **Marinate:**
   - Cover the jar with a lid and refrigerate for at least 24 hours, preferably 48 hours or more, to allow the flavors to develop and the eggs to absorb the color.
5. **Serve:**
   - Once marinated to your liking, remove the red beet eggs from the brine. They can be served whole or sliced. Enjoy them as a colorful and tangy addition to salads, as a side dish, or as a snack.

Tips:

- **Peeling Eggs:** For easier peeling of hard-boiled eggs, use eggs that are not too fresh. You can also add a little vinegar or baking soda to the boiling water to help with peeling.
- **Customization:** Feel free to adjust the sweetness or tanginess of the brine by varying the amount of sugar and vinegar to suit your taste.
- **Storage:** Store leftover red beet eggs in the refrigerator in their brine for up to 1 week. The longer they marinate, the more flavorful they become.

Red beet eggs are not only delicious but also add a vibrant touch to any table. They are a unique and traditional dish that's beloved for its tangy-sweet flavor and eye-catching appearance. Enjoy making and sharing these Pennsylvania Dutch treats!

Baked Apples

Ingredients:

- 4 large apples (such as Granny Smith, Honeycrisp, or Gala)
- 1/4 cup brown sugar or granulated sugar
- 1 tsp ground cinnamon
- 1/4 tsp ground nutmeg
- 1/4 cup chopped nuts (such as pecans or walnuts), optional
- 2 tbsp unsalted butter, cut into small cubes
- 1/2 cup apple cider or apple juice (or water)

Instructions:

1. **Preheat Oven:**
    - Preheat your oven to 375°F (190°C).
2. **Prepare Apples:**
    - Wash the apples thoroughly. Using a paring knife or an apple corer, carefully remove the cores from the apples, leaving the bottoms intact to form a cavity for the filling.
3. **Mix Filling:**
    - In a small bowl, mix together the brown sugar (or granulated sugar), ground cinnamon, ground nutmeg, and chopped nuts (if using).
4. **Fill Apples:**
    - Place the cored apples upright in a baking dish. Divide the filling mixture evenly among the apples, stuffing it into the cavities. Top each apple with cubes of butter.
5. **Bake:**
    - Pour apple cider or apple juice (or water) into the bottom of the baking dish around the apples. This helps to keep them moist and adds flavor.
    - Bake in the preheated oven for 30-40 minutes, or until the apples are tender and can be easily pierced with a fork.
6. **Baste:**
    - Occasionally during baking, spoon some of the juices from the bottom of the baking dish over the tops of the apples to keep them moist and flavorful.
7. **Serve:**
    - Remove the baked apples from the oven. Serve them warm, optionally with a scoop of vanilla ice cream or a dollop of whipped cream. Drizzle with any remaining juices from the baking dish.

Tips:

- **Variations:** Experiment with different fillings such as raisins, dried cranberries, or chopped dates. You can also add a splash of vanilla extract or a pinch of cloves for additional flavor.
- **Storage:** Baked apples are best enjoyed fresh from the oven. However, you can store any leftovers in the refrigerator for up to 2 days. Reheat gently in the microwave or oven before serving.

Baked apples are a comforting and versatile dessert that's perfect for fall and winter. They are simple to make and can be customized to suit your taste preferences. Enjoy the warm, spiced aroma that fills your kitchen as they bake!

Beef Stew

Ingredients:

- 2 lbs beef stew meat, cut into 1-inch cubes
- Salt and pepper, to taste
- 1/4 cup all-purpose flour
- 2-3 tbsp vegetable oil or olive oil
- 1 large onion, chopped
- 3-4 cloves garlic, minced
- 4 cups beef broth
- 1 cup red wine (optional; can substitute with additional beef broth or water)
- 2 tbsp tomato paste
- 1 tbsp Worcestershire sauce
- 1 tsp dried thyme
- 1 tsp dried rosemary
- 2 bay leaves
- 4 medium potatoes, peeled and cut into chunks
- 4 carrots, peeled and cut into chunks
- 2 celery stalks, chopped
- 1 cup frozen peas (optional)
- Chopped fresh parsley, for garnish (optional)

Instructions:

1. **Prepare the Beef:**
    - Pat the beef cubes dry with paper towels. Season generously with salt and pepper. Coat the beef cubes with flour, shaking off any excess.
2. **Brown the Beef:**
    - In a large Dutch oven or heavy-bottomed pot, heat 2 tablespoons of oil over medium-high heat. Working in batches to avoid overcrowding, brown the beef cubes on all sides. Transfer the browned beef to a plate and set aside.
3. **Saute Onions and Garlic:**
    - Add the chopped onions to the same pot and sauté until softened, about 5-6 minutes. Add minced garlic and cook for another minute until fragrant.
4. **Deglaze the Pot:**
    - Pour in the red wine (if using), scraping the bottom of the pot with a wooden spoon to loosen any browned bits (this adds flavor to the stew). Let the wine simmer for a few minutes until slightly reduced.
5. **Add Broth and Seasonings:**
    - Return the browned beef cubes to the pot. Add beef broth, tomato paste, Worcestershire sauce, dried thyme, dried rosemary, and bay leaves. Stir to combine. Bring the mixture to a boil, then reduce the heat to low. Cover and simmer for 1.5 to 2 hours, or until the beef is tender.

6. **Add Vegetables:**
   - Add the potatoes, carrots, and celery to the pot. Cover and simmer for another 30-45 minutes, or until the vegetables are tender and the stew has thickened to your liking.
7. **Add Peas (if using) and Adjust Seasoning:**
   - If using frozen peas, add them to the stew during the last 5-10 minutes of cooking. Taste and adjust seasoning with salt and pepper as needed.
8. **Serve:**
   - Remove the bay leaves before serving. Ladle the beef stew into bowls and garnish with chopped fresh parsley, if desired. Serve hot, accompanied by crusty bread or over cooked rice or mashed potatoes.

Tips:

- **Slow Cooker Method:** Alternatively, you can cook beef stew in a slow cooker. Follow steps 1-4 to brown the beef and sauté the onions and garlic. Transfer everything to a slow cooker, add remaining ingredients (except peas), and cook on low for 7-8 hours or on high for 3-4 hours.
- **Beef Selection:** For best results, use beef stew meat that has marbled fat, such as chuck roast or bottom round, as they become tender and flavorful when cooked slowly.
- **Make-Ahead:** Beef stew tastes even better the next day as the flavors meld together. It can be refrigerated for up to 3 days or frozen for longer storage.

This classic beef stew recipe yields a hearty and comforting dish that's perfect for family meals or gatherings. Enjoy the rich flavors and tender beef in every spoonful!

Amish Cheese Ball

Ingredients:

- 8 oz cream cheese, softened
- 2 cups shredded cheddar cheese
- 1/4 cup grated Parmesan cheese
- 1/4 cup mayonnaise
- 1 tbsp Worcestershire sauce
- 1 tsp garlic powder
- 1/2 tsp onion powder
- 1/4 tsp smoked paprika (optional)
- Salt and pepper, to taste
- 1 cup chopped pecans or walnuts, toasted
- Chopped fresh parsley or chives, for garnish (optional)
- Crackers, for serving

Instructions:

1. **Mix Cheese Base:**
   - In a large mixing bowl, combine softened cream cheese, shredded cheddar cheese, grated Parmesan cheese, mayonnaise, Worcestershire sauce, garlic powder, onion powder, smoked paprika (if using), salt, and pepper. Use a spatula or electric mixer to blend everything together until smooth and well combined.
2. **Shape the Cheese Ball:**
   - Once the mixture is well combined, shape it into a ball. Use plastic wrap or parchment paper to help shape and roll the cheese mixture into a smooth ball.
3. **Coat with Nuts:**
   - Spread the chopped pecans or walnuts on a flat plate or baking sheet. Roll the cheese ball in the nuts, pressing gently to coat the entire surface evenly.
4. **Chill:**
   - Wrap the coated cheese ball in plastic wrap and refrigerate for at least 1 hour, or until firm. Chilling helps the flavors to meld together and makes the cheese ball easier to handle.
5. **Garnish and Serve:**
   - Before serving, optionally garnish the cheese ball with chopped fresh parsley or chives for added color and freshness. Serve chilled with crackers for dipping.

Tips:

- **Variations:** Feel free to customize the cheese ball by adding chopped green onions, minced garlic, or even crumbled cooked bacon for extra flavor.
- **Make-Ahead:** You can prepare the cheese ball up to 2 days in advance. Keep it wrapped in plastic wrap and stored in the refrigerator until ready to serve.

- **Serve with:** Amish cheese ball pairs well with assorted crackers, breadsticks, or vegetable sticks for dipping.

This Amish cheese ball is sure to be a hit at parties or gatherings with its creamy texture and savory flavors. Enjoy making and sharing this delicious appetizer with friends and family!

Shaker Chicken and Dumplings

Ingredients:

For the Chicken Stew:

- 2 lbs bone-in, skin-on chicken thighs or breasts
- Salt and pepper, to taste
- 2 tbsp vegetable oil or butter
- 1 onion, chopped
- 3 carrots, peeled and sliced
- 3 celery stalks, sliced
- 3 cloves garlic, minced
- 6 cups chicken broth
- 1 bay leaf
- 1 tsp dried thyme
- 1 tsp dried parsley
- 1/2 cup heavy cream (optional, for richness)

For the Dumplings:

- 2 cups all-purpose flour
- 1 tbsp baking powder
- 1/2 tsp salt
- 1/2 cup unsalted butter, chilled and cut into small pieces
- 3/4 cup milk

Instructions:

1. **Cook the Chicken:**
   - Season the chicken pieces with salt and pepper. In a large Dutch oven or pot, heat the vegetable oil or butter over medium-high heat. Brown the chicken on both sides until golden, about 4-5 minutes per side. Remove the chicken and set aside.
2. **Saute Vegetables:**
   - In the same pot, add the chopped onion, carrots, and celery. Cook until the vegetables begin to soften, about 5 minutes. Add the minced garlic and cook for another minute until fragrant.
3. **Simmer the Stew:**
   - Return the browned chicken to the pot. Add the chicken broth, bay leaf, dried thyme, and dried parsley. Bring to a boil, then reduce the heat to low. Cover and simmer for 30-40 minutes, or until the chicken is cooked through and tender.
4. **Prepare Dumpling Dough:**
   - While the stew simmers, prepare the dumplings. In a mixing bowl, whisk together the flour, baking powder, and salt. Cut in the chilled butter using a pastry cutter or

fork until the mixture resembles coarse crumbs. Stir in the milk until just combined.

5. **Add Dumplings to Stew:**
   - After the chicken is cooked, remove it from the pot and shred it into bite-sized pieces using two forks. Return the shredded chicken to the pot. Increase the heat to medium-high and bring the stew to a gentle simmer.

6. **Form and Cook Dumplings:**
   - Drop spoonfuls of the dumpling dough onto the simmering stew, making sure they are evenly distributed. Cover the pot with a lid and simmer for 15-20 minutes, or until the dumplings are cooked through and fluffy.

7. **Finish with Cream (optional):**
   - If using heavy cream for richness, stir it into the stew after the dumplings have cooked. Simmer for an additional 5 minutes to heat through. Taste and adjust seasoning with salt and pepper if needed.

8. **Serve:**
   - Ladle the Shaker chicken and dumplings into bowls. Garnish with chopped fresh parsley if desired. Serve hot and enjoy the comforting flavors of this rustic dish.

Tips:

- **Vegetable Variations:** Feel free to add peas, corn, or mushrooms to the stew for added texture and flavor.
- **Make-Ahead:** The stew can be prepared ahead of time and stored in the refrigerator for up to 2 days. Add the dumplings just before serving.
- **Leftovers:** Leftover chicken and dumplings can be stored in an airtight container in the refrigerator for 2-3 days. Reheat gently on the stove or in the microwave before serving.

This Shaker-inspired chicken and dumplings recipe is hearty, comforting, and perfect for a cozy family dinner. Enjoy the warmth and satisfaction of homemade comfort food with this timeless dish!

Black Raspberry Jam

Ingredients:

- 4 cups fresh black raspberries (about 1.5 lbs)
- 4 cups granulated sugar
- 1/4 cup fresh lemon juice
- 1 package (1.75 oz) powdered fruit pectin

Instructions:

1. **Prepare the Berries:**
   - Rinse the black raspberries under cold water and remove any stems or leaves. Crush the berries using a potato masher or a fork until you have a chunky consistency. Measure out 4 cups of crushed berries.
2. **Combine Ingredients:**
   - In a large, heavy-bottomed pot, combine the crushed black raspberries and lemon juice. Gradually stir in the powdered fruit pectin until it's fully dissolved.
3. **Cook the Jam:**
   - Over medium-high heat, bring the berry mixture to a full rolling boil (a boil that doesn't stop bubbling when stirred). Stir in the granulated sugar all at once. Return the mixture to a full rolling boil, stirring constantly. Boil hard for 1 minute, continuing to stir.
4. **Test for Gel Point:**
   - To test if the jam has reached the gel point (where it will set properly), use a candy thermometer or perform a gel test. For the gel test, place a small amount of the hot jam on a chilled plate and let it cool for a minute. Push the edge of the jam with your fingertip; if it wrinkles and feels thickened, it's ready.
5. **Remove from Heat and Skim Foam:**
   - Once the jam has reached the desired consistency, remove it from the heat. Skim off any foam that has formed on the surface with a spoon.
6. **Can the Jam:**
   - Ladle the hot jam into sterilized jars, leaving about 1/4-inch headspace. Wipe the jar rims clean with a damp cloth. Place sterilized lids on the jars and screw on the bands until fingertip tight.
7. **Process the Jars (Optional):**
   - If you want to store the jam long-term at room temperature, process the jars in a boiling water bath for 10 minutes (adjust time for altitude if necessary). Alternatively, store the jars in the refrigerator once cooled.
8. **Cool and Store:**
   - Let the jars cool completely at room temperature. Check the seals after 24 hours; lids should not flex up and down when the center is pressed. Label and store in a cool, dark place.

Tips:

- **Raspberries:** If you can't find black raspberries, you can use regular red raspberries for a slightly different flavor.
- **Pectin:** Follow the package instructions for the specific type of pectin you use, as the amount needed may vary.
- **Consistency:** Jam will continue to thicken as it cools, so don't overcook it.
- **Storage:** Properly canned jam can be stored in a cool, dark place for up to 1 year. Once opened, store in the refrigerator for up to 3 weeks.

Homemade black raspberry jam is perfect spread on toast, biscuits, or used in desserts. Enjoy the rich, fruity flavor of this delightful preserve!

Pumpkin Whoopie Pies

Ingredients:

For the Pumpkin Cookies:

- 2 cups all-purpose flour
- 1 tsp baking powder
- 1 tsp baking soda
- 1 tsp ground cinnamon
- 1/2 tsp ground ginger
- 1/4 tsp ground nutmeg
- 1/4 tsp ground cloves
- 1/2 tsp salt
- 1/2 cup unsalted butter, softened
- 1 cup packed light brown sugar
- 1 large egg
- 1 cup canned pumpkin puree
- 1 tsp vanilla extract

For the Cream Cheese Filling:

- 8 oz cream cheese, softened
- 1/2 cup unsalted butter, softened
- 2 cups powdered sugar
- 1 tsp vanilla extract

Instructions:

1. **Make the Pumpkin Cookies:**
    - Preheat your oven to 350°F (175°C). Line baking sheets with parchment paper or silicone mats.
    - In a medium bowl, whisk together the flour, baking powder, baking soda, cinnamon, ginger, nutmeg, cloves, and salt until well combined.
    - In a large bowl or the bowl of a stand mixer, beat together the softened butter and brown sugar until light and fluffy. Add the egg and beat until well combined. Mix in the pumpkin puree and vanilla extract.
    - Gradually add the dry ingredients to the wet ingredients, mixing until just combined and no streaks of flour remain.
    - Drop tablespoon-sized portions of dough onto the prepared baking sheets, spacing them about 2 inches apart.
    - Bake in the preheated oven for 10-12 minutes, or until the cookies are set and slightly firm to the touch. Remove from the oven and let cool on the baking sheets for a few minutes before transferring them to a wire rack to cool completely.

2. **Make the Cream Cheese Filling:**
   - In a medium bowl, beat together the softened cream cheese and butter until smooth and creamy.
   - Gradually add the powdered sugar, beating well after each addition, until the filling is smooth and fluffy. Mix in the vanilla extract.
3. **Assemble the Whoopie Pies:**
   - Match up the cooled pumpkin cookies in pairs of similar size.
   - Spread a generous amount of the cream cheese filling onto the flat side of one cookie in each pair.
   - Top with the flat side of the second cookie, pressing gently to spread the filling evenly to the edges.
4. **Serve and Store:**
   - Serve the pumpkin whoopie pies immediately, or store them in an airtight container in the refrigerator. They taste best after chilling for a few hours to allow the flavors to meld.

Tips:

- **Pumpkin Puree:** Use canned pumpkin puree for consistent results. Make sure it's not pumpkin pie filling, which has added spices and sugar.
- **Spice Variations:** Adjust the spices to your taste preferences. You can increase the amount of cinnamon or add a pinch of ground cloves for extra flavor.
- **Storage:** Whoopie pies can be stored in the refrigerator for up to 3-4 days. Bring them to room temperature before serving for the best texture.

These pumpkin whoopie pies are a perfect blend of moist pumpkin cookies and creamy filling, making them a delightful treat for any occasion, especially during the autumn season. Enjoy sharing these with family and friends!

Amish Wedding Cake

Ingredients:

- 1 cup unsalted butter, softened
- 2 cups granulated sugar
- 4 large eggs
- 3 cups all-purpose flour
- 1/2 tsp baking soda
- 1/2 tsp salt
- 1 tsp ground cinnamon
- 1/2 tsp ground nutmeg
- 1/2 tsp ground allspice
- 1 cup sour cream
- 1 cup chopped nuts (such as pecans or walnuts)
- 1 cup mixed dried fruits (such as raisins, currants, chopped apricots, and dates)
- 1/2 cup candied fruit (such as candied cherries or citron), optional
- 1/2 cup brandy or rum (optional, for soaking the dried fruits)
- Powdered sugar, for dusting (optional)

Instructions:

1. **Prepare the Dried Fruits (if soaking):**
   - In a small bowl, combine the mixed dried fruits and candied fruit (if using) with brandy or rum. Let them soak for at least 1 hour, or preferably overnight, to plump up and absorb the flavors.
2. **Preheat Oven and Prepare Pan:**
   - Preheat your oven to 325°F (160°C). Grease and flour a Bundt pan or tube pan, or line it with parchment paper for easier removal.
3. **Cream Butter and Sugar:**
   - In a large mixing bowl, cream together the softened butter and granulated sugar until light and fluffy, using an electric mixer or stand mixer.
4. **Add Eggs and Dry Ingredients:**
   - Add the eggs one at a time, mixing well after each addition.
5. **Combine Dry Ingredients:**
   - In a separate bowl, sift together the flour, baking soda, salt, cinnamon, nutmeg, and allspice.
6. **Alternate Mixing:**
   - Gradually add the dry ingredients to the butter-sugar mixture, alternating with the sour cream. Begin and end with the flour mixture, mixing until just combined.
7. **Fold in Nuts and Fruits:**
   - Fold in the chopped nuts and soaked dried fruits (including any soaking liquid) until evenly distributed throughout the batter.
8. **Bake:**

- Pour the batter into the prepared pan, spreading it evenly. Bake in the preheated oven for 1 hour to 1 hour 15 minutes, or until a toothpick inserted into the center comes out clean.

9. **Cool and Serve:**
   - Allow the cake to cool in the pan for about 10 minutes before transferring it to a wire rack to cool completely. Once cooled, dust with powdered sugar if desired.

Tips:

- **Soaking Fruits:** Soaking the dried fruits in brandy or rum adds moisture and flavor to the cake. If preferred, you can substitute with orange juice or apple juice for a non-alcoholic version.
- **Storage:** Store the Amish wedding cake in an airtight container at room temperature for up to 5 days. It also freezes well; wrap tightly in plastic wrap and store in an airtight container for up to 3 months.

This Amish wedding cake is a wonderful dessert option that celebrates the rich flavors of dried fruits and nuts. It's perfect for festive occasions or as a special treat to share with loved ones. Enjoy baking and savoring this classic Amish delicacy!

Scalloped Corn

Ingredients:

- 4 cups fresh or canned corn kernels (about 4 ears of corn)
- 1/2 cup milk
- 2 eggs, beaten
- 1/4 cup unsalted butter, melted
- 1/4 cup granulated sugar
- 1/4 cup all-purpose flour
- 1/2 tsp salt
- 1/4 tsp ground black pepper
- 1 cup shredded cheddar cheese
- 1 cup crushed butter crackers (such as Ritz) or breadcrumbs

Instructions:

1. **Preheat Oven:**
   - Preheat your oven to 350°F (175°C). Grease a 9x9-inch baking dish or a similar-sized casserole dish.
2. **Prepare Corn:**
   - If using fresh corn, cut the kernels off the cob. If using canned corn, drain well.
3. **Mix Ingredients:**
   - In a large mixing bowl, combine the corn kernels, milk, beaten eggs, melted butter, sugar, flour, salt, pepper, and shredded cheddar cheese. Stir well until all ingredients are evenly combined.
4. **Transfer to Baking Dish:**
   - Pour the corn mixture into the greased baking dish, spreading it out evenly.
5. **Add Topping:**
   - Sprinkle the crushed butter crackers or breadcrumbs evenly over the top of the corn mixture.
6. **Bake:**
   - Bake in the preheated oven for 45-50 minutes, or until the top is golden brown and the center is set. The edges should be bubbling slightly.
7. **Serve:**
   - Remove from the oven and let it cool for a few minutes before serving. Serve warm as a side dish.

Tips:

- **Variations:** Add diced bell peppers, jalapeños, or cooked bacon for additional flavor and texture.
- **Cheese Options:** Feel free to use other types of cheese such as Monterey Jack or a blend of cheeses for a different flavor profile.

- **Make-Ahead:** You can assemble the scalloped corn ahead of time and refrigerate it (without baking) for up to 24 hours. Bake it just before serving.
- **Leftovers:** Store leftovers in an airtight container in the refrigerator for up to 3 days. Reheat in the oven or microwave before serving.

This scalloped corn recipe is creamy, cheesy, and comforting—a perfect addition to any meal, especially during the cooler months or for holiday gatherings. Enjoy the rich flavors and creamy texture of this classic side dish!

Chicken Fingers

Ingredients:

- 1 lb chicken breasts, boneless and skinless
- 1 cup all-purpose flour
- 2 large eggs, beaten
- 1 cup breadcrumbs (plain or seasoned)
- 1/2 cup grated Parmesan cheese (optional, for extra flavor)
- 1 tsp salt, divided
- 1/2 tsp black pepper
- 1/2 tsp paprika
- Vegetable oil, for frying

Instructions:

1. **Prepare the Chicken:**
   - Cut the chicken breasts into strips about 1 inch wide and 3-4 inches long. Season the chicken strips with 1/2 tsp salt and black pepper.
2. **Set Up Breading Station:**
   - Prepare three shallow bowls or plates. Place the flour in one bowl, beaten eggs in another bowl, and breadcrumbs mixed with Parmesan cheese (if using), paprika, and remaining 1/2 tsp salt in the third bowl.
3. **Bread the Chicken Strips:**
   - Dredge each chicken strip in the flour, shaking off any excess.
   - Dip the floured chicken strip into the beaten eggs, ensuring it's evenly coated.
   - Finally, coat the chicken strip in the breadcrumb mixture, pressing gently to adhere the breadcrumbs.
4. **Fry the Chicken Fingers:**
   - In a large skillet or frying pan, heat about 1/2 inch of vegetable oil over medium-high heat until it reaches 350°F (175°C).
   - Carefully place the breaded chicken strips in the hot oil, in batches if necessary to avoid overcrowding the pan. Cook for about 3-4 minutes per side, or until golden brown and cooked through. The internal temperature of the chicken should reach 165°F (74°C).
5. **Drain and Serve:**
   - Remove the cooked chicken fingers from the oil and place them on a plate lined with paper towels to drain excess oil.
6. **Serve with Dipping Sauces:**
   - Serve the chicken fingers hot, with your favorite dipping sauces such as ketchup, honey mustard, barbecue sauce, or ranch dressing.

Tips:

- **Oven-Baked Option:** For a healthier alternative, you can bake the breaded chicken fingers in a preheated oven at 400°F (200°C) for about 15-20 minutes, flipping halfway through, until they are golden and cooked through.
- **Freezing:** You can freeze breaded, uncooked chicken fingers on a baking sheet until solid, then transfer them to a freezer bag for up to 3 months. Fry or bake them directly from frozen, adding a few extra minutes to the cooking time.

Homemade chicken fingers are versatile and can be enjoyed as a main dish, appetizer, or even as a part of a packed lunch. They're sure to be a hit with both kids and adults alike!

Rhubarb Custard Pie

Ingredients:

For the Pie Crust:

- 1 1/4 cups all-purpose flour
- 1/2 tsp salt
- 1/2 cup unsalted butter, cold and cut into small cubes
- 3-4 tbsp ice water

For the Filling:

- 3 cups rhubarb, chopped into 1/2-inch pieces
- 1 1/4 cups granulated sugar
- 1/4 cup all-purpose flour
- 3 large eggs
- 1 cup heavy cream
- 1 tsp vanilla extract
- 1/4 tsp ground nutmeg
- 1/4 tsp ground cinnamon

Instructions:

1. **Prepare the Pie Crust:**
   - In a large mixing bowl, whisk together the flour and salt. Add the cold butter cubes and use a pastry cutter or fork to cut the butter into the flour until the mixture resembles coarse crumbs.
   - Gradually add the ice water, 1 tablespoon at a time, mixing gently with a fork until the dough just holds together when squeezed with your fingers. Be careful not to overmix.
   - Shape the dough into a disk, wrap it in plastic wrap, and refrigerate for at least 30 minutes.
2. **Preheat Oven:**
   - Preheat your oven to 400°F (200°C).
3. **Roll Out the Dough:**
   - On a lightly floured surface, roll out the chilled pie crust dough into a circle about 12 inches in diameter. Transfer the dough to a 9-inch pie dish, gently pressing it into the bottom and up the sides. Trim any excess dough and crimp the edges decoratively. Refrigerate while you prepare the filling.
4. **Prepare the Filling:**
   - In a large mixing bowl, combine the chopped rhubarb, granulated sugar, and flour. Toss to coat the rhubarb evenly.
   - In another bowl, whisk together the eggs, heavy cream, vanilla extract, nutmeg, and cinnamon until well combined.

- Pour the egg mixture over the rhubarb mixture and gently stir until everything is evenly coated.
5. **Assemble and Bake:**
    - Pour the rhubarb custard filling into the prepared pie crust.
    - Place the pie on a baking sheet (to catch any spills) and bake in the preheated oven for 10 minutes. Reduce the oven temperature to 350°F (175°C) and continue baking for 45-50 minutes, or until the filling is set and the crust is golden brown.
6. **Cool and Serve:**
    - Remove the pie from the oven and let it cool completely on a wire rack before slicing and serving.

Tips:

- **Rhubarb Prep:** If using fresh rhubarb, be sure to trim off any leaves (which are toxic) and chop the stalks into uniform pieces for even cooking.
- **Custard Consistency:** The custard should be set but still slightly jiggly in the center when the pie is done baking. It will continue to firm up as it cools.
- **Serve with:** Rhubarb custard pie is delicious on its own but can be served with a dollop of whipped cream or a scoop of vanilla ice cream for an extra treat.

This rhubarb custard pie combines the tangy flavor of rhubarb with the creamy richness of custard, all encased in a flaky, buttery crust. It's a perfect dessert to celebrate rhubarb season or any special occasion!

Sloppy Joes

Ingredients:

- 1 lb (450g) ground beef
- 1 small onion, finely chopped
- 1 small green bell pepper, finely chopped
- 2 cloves garlic, minced
- 1 cup ketchup
- 2 tablespoons tomato paste
- 1 tablespoon brown sugar (adjust to taste)
- 1 tablespoon Worcestershire sauce
- 1 teaspoon mustard (preferably Dijon)
- 1/2 teaspoon chili powder (adjust to taste)
- Salt and pepper to taste
- Hamburger buns

Instructions:

1. **Cook the beef:** In a large skillet or frying pan, cook the ground beef over medium-high heat until browned and cooked through. Break up the beef into crumbles as it cooks. Drain excess fat if necessary.
2. **Add vegetables:** Add the chopped onion, green pepper, and minced garlic to the skillet with the beef. Cook for 3-4 minutes until the vegetables are softened.
3. **Make the sauce:** Stir in the ketchup, tomato paste, brown sugar, Worcestershire sauce, mustard, chili powder, salt, and pepper. Reduce heat to medium-low and let simmer for 10-15 minutes, stirring occasionally, until the sauce thickens slightly and the flavors meld together. Taste and adjust seasoning as needed.
4. **Serve:** Spoon the Sloppy Joe mixture onto hamburger buns, and serve hot.
5. **Optional toppings:** You can serve Sloppy Joes with cheese slices, pickles, or coleslaw for extra flavor and texture.

Enjoy your homemade Sloppy Joes! They're great for a quick and satisfying meal.

Amish Macaroni Salad

Ingredients:

- 2 cups elbow macaroni
- 1 cup mayonnaise
- 2 tablespoons white vinegar
- 2 tablespoons sugar
- 1 tablespoon Dijon mustard
- 1 teaspoon salt
- 1/2 teaspoon black pepper
- 1/2 cup celery, finely chopped
- 1/2 cup red bell pepper, finely chopped
- 1/2 cup green bell pepper, finely chopped
- 1/4 cup red onion, finely chopped
- 2 hard-boiled eggs, chopped
- Optional: 1/2 cup sweet pickles, chopped (for a sweeter variation)

Instructions:

1. **Cook the macaroni:** Cook the elbow macaroni according to package instructions until al dente. Drain and rinse under cold water to cool down the pasta. Drain well and set aside.
2. **Prepare the dressing:** In a large bowl, whisk together the mayonnaise, white vinegar, sugar, Dijon mustard, salt, and black pepper until smooth and well combined.
3. **Combine ingredients:** Add the cooled macaroni to the bowl with the dressing. Add the celery, red bell pepper, green bell pepper, red onion, chopped eggs, and sweet pickles (if using). Gently toss everything together until the macaroni and vegetables are evenly coated with the dressing.
4. **Chill and serve:** Cover the bowl with plastic wrap and refrigerate for at least 2 hours (or overnight) to allow the flavors to meld together.
5. **Serve:** Before serving, give the macaroni salad a gentle stir. Taste and adjust seasoning if needed. Serve chilled.

This Amish Macaroni Salad is perfect for picnics, potlucks, or as a side dish for barbecues. Enjoy!

Baked Chicken

Ingredients:

- 4 boneless, skinless chicken breasts (or thighs, if preferred)
- 2 tablespoons olive oil
- 2 cloves garlic, minced
- 1 teaspoon paprika
- 1 teaspoon dried thyme (or any dried herb of your choice, such as rosemary or oregano)
- 1/2 teaspoon salt
- 1/4 teaspoon black pepper
- Optional: lemon slices, fresh herbs (like parsley or thyme) for garnish

Instructions:

1. **Preheat the oven:** Preheat your oven to 400°F (200°C).
2. **Prepare the chicken:** Pat the chicken breasts dry with paper towels. Place them in a baking dish or on a baking sheet lined with parchment paper.
3. **Season the chicken:** In a small bowl, mix together the olive oil, minced garlic, paprika, dried thyme, salt, and black pepper. Brush or drizzle this mixture evenly over both sides of the chicken breasts.
4. **Bake the chicken:** Place the baking dish in the preheated oven. Bake for about 20-25 minutes, or until the chicken is cooked through and reaches an internal temperature of 165°F (74°C). Cooking time may vary depending on the thickness of your chicken breasts.
5. **Rest and serve:** Once baked, remove the chicken from the oven and let it rest for a few minutes. This allows the juices to redistribute and ensures tender, juicy chicken. Optionally, garnish with lemon slices and fresh herbs before serving.
6. **Serve:** Serve the baked chicken hot with your favorite sides, such as roasted vegetables, salad, or rice.

This baked chicken recipe is straightforward and produces flavorful, moist chicken that's perfect for a quick and satisfying meal. Enjoy!